# GASTRIC SLEEVE BARIATRIC COOKBOOK

365 DAYS OF BARIATRIC WARRIOR DIET TO SEND YOUR FOOD ADDICTION TO HELL AND AVOID REGAINING WEIGHT AFTER SURGERY WITH STRATEGIC RECIPES & A TESTED 12-WEEK MEAL PLAN

© COPYRIGHT 2021 - ALL RIGHTS RESERVED.

This document is geared towards providing exact and reliable information in regard to the topic and issue covered.

- From a Declaration of Principles which was accepted and approved equally by a Committee of the American Bar Association and a Committee of Publishers and Associations.

In no way is it legal to reproduce, duplicate, or transmit any part of this document in either electronic means or in printed format. All rights reserved.

The information provided herein is stated to be truthful and consistent, in that any liability, in terms of inattention or otherwise, by any usage or abuse of any policies, processes, or directions contained within is the solitary and utter responsibility of the recipient reader. Under no circumstances will any legal responsibility or blame be held against the publisher for any reparation, damages, or monetary loss due to the information herein, either directly or indirectly.

Respective authors own all copyrights not held by the publisher.

The information herein is offered for informational purposes solely and is universal as so. The presentation of the information is without contract or any type of guarantee assurance.

The trademarks that are used are without any consent, and the publication of the trademark is without permission or backing by the trademark owner. All trademarks and brands within this book are for clarifying purposes only and are owned by the owners themselves, not affiliated with this document.

# Table of Contents

**INTRODUCTION** ..................................................9

**CHAPTER 1: THE BASICS OF THE BARIATRIC DIET** ..................................................11
- Difference between Gastric Sleeve and Gastric Bypass..................................................10
- Benefits of Gastric Sleeve Bariatric Surgery.....10

**CHAPTER 2: MENTAL APPROACH TO THE DISORDER, DEVELOPING RESILIENCE** .......14
- Tips for Boosting Your Resiliency ....................15

**CHAPTER 3: BARIATRIC LIFESTYLE** ................................................. 16
- Before the Surgery............................................17
- How Does Gastric Sleeve Surgery Work?...........17
- After the Surgery..............................................17
- Complications After Surgery?..........................17
- Stages of Diet...................................................17
- Food Cravings..................................................18
- Foods to Eat and Avoid After Surgery................18
- Types of Diets...................................................18
- Reinforced Gastric Sleeve.................................18
- Virtual Gastric Sleeve.......................................18

**CHAPTER 4: LIQUID RECIPES MEAL PREP FOR FIRST 2 WEEKS** ..................................20
- WEEK 1............................................................21
- Week 2...............................................................1

**CHAPTER 5: MEAL PREP PUREED AND SOFT RECIPES FOR 4 WEEKS** ..............................22
- Week 1..............................................................23
- Week 2..............................................................23
- Week 3..............................................................24
- Week 4..............................................................24

**CHAPTER 6: FOOD PREP GENERAL DIET FOR 6 WEEKS** ..................................................25
- Week 1..............................................................26
- Week 2..............................................................26
- Week 3..............................................................27
- Week 4..............................................................27
- Week 5..............................................................28
- Week 6..............................................................28

**CHAPTER 7: EMOTIONAL RESILIENCE AND MEDITATION EXERCISES** ........................ 29

**CHAPTER 8: LIQUID RECIPES** .................... 32
- 1. Alcohol-Free Mint Mojito ..............................33
- 2. Sugar-Free Strawberry Limeade....................33
- 3. Hearty Mint Tea ............................................33
- 4. Orange and Apricot Juice ..............................33
- 5. Apple and Citrus Juice ..................................34
- 6. Blueberry Cacao Blast ..................................34
- 7. Cucumber and Avocado Dill Smoothie ..........34
- Guided Meditation 1........................................34
- 8. Spinach Green Smoothie...............................35

9. Coco-Banana Milkshake ........................35
10. Strawberry and Cherry Shake .............35
11. Chia Blueberry Banana Oatmeal Smoothie ...... 35
12. Banana-Cherry Smoothie......................35
13. Mango Smoothie....................................36
14. Cashew Milk ..........................................36
15. Pumpkin and carrot soup.....................36
Guided Meditation 2......................................36

## CHAPTER 9: PUREED AND SOFT RECIPES .................................................. 40

16. Apple Cinnamon Protein Oatmeal ......41
17. Apple Parfait ..........................................41
19. Blackberry Muffins ...............................42
20. Butternut Squash, Cashew and Turkey Puree ..........................................................42
21. Roasted Cauliflower Fritters................43
22. Spicy Ground Beef Rolls......................43
23. Chicken Apple Zucchini Puree ............43
24. Chocolate Parfait ..................................44
Guided Meditation 3......................................44
25. Oatmeal Cookie Shake ........................45
26. Scrambled Eggs with Black Bean Puree ......45
27. Frozen Mocha Frappuccino ................45
28. Black Bean and Lime Puree ................46
29. Chocolate PB2 Banana Protein Shake ........46
30. Pumpkin Protein Smoothie..................46
31. Apple Cucumber Juice .........................46
32. Vitamin C Juice .....................................47
33. Cherry Mango Smoothie......................47
34. Coco-Rita Cocktail ................................47
Guided Meditation 4......................................47

## CHAPTER 10: BREAKFAST ........................52

35. Berry Cheesecake Overnight Oats .............53
36. Pumpkin Protein Pancakes .........................53
37. Avocado Toast with Cottage Cheese & Tomatoes ..................................................................53
38. Savory Parmesan Oatmeal .........................53
39. Strawberry Cheesecake Chia Seed Pudding ...
..........................................................................54
40. Mocha banana protein smoothie bowl .........54
41. Apple Pie Oatmeal .......................................54
42. Pumpkin Apple French Toast Bake ............55
43. Blueberry Greek Yogurt Pancakes ............55
44. Blackberry Almond Butter Sandwich ..........55
45. Blackberry Vanilla French Toast .................56
46. Chocolate-Peanut Butter French Toast ......56
Guided Meditation 5........................................56
47. Watermelon Quinoa Parfait .......................58
48. Apple and Goat Cheese Sandwich .............58
49. Carrot Cake Oatmeal ..................................58
50. Coconut Cranberry Protein Bars .................59
51. Egg white Oatmeal with Strawberries and Peanut Butter ..................................................59
52. Avocado Shrimp Salad ...............................59
53. Easy Baked Salmon ....................................59
54. Mushroom Strata and Turkey Sausage ......60
55. Millet Congee ..............................................60
56. Avocado Cherry Smoothie .........................61
57. Quinoa Bowls ..............................................61
58. Berry Muesli ................................................61
59. Vanilla Egg Custard ....................................61
60. Asparagus Omelet ......................................62
61. Strawberry & Mushroom Sandwich ...........62
Guided Meditation 6........................................62

## CHAPTER 11: SOUPS AND SALADS ............66

62. Ham & Bean..................................................67
63. Frank Sinatra Soup......................................67
64. Orange Fidelity............................................67
65. Potato Broccoli Soup...................................68
66. Creamy Chicken Vegetable Soup................68
67. Clam Chowder.............................................69
68. Cream of Broccoli Soup ..............................69
69. Chicken Noodle Soup..................................69
70. Corn and Black Bean Salad.........................70
71. Seven Layer Mexican Salad........................70
72. Chipotle Steak Salad...................................71
73. Soft Mexican Chicken Salad........................71
74. Caprese Salad Bites....................................71
75. Greek Chop-Chop Salad..............................72
Guided Meditation 7.........................................72

## CHAPTER 12: SIDES AND SNACKS ............76

76. Strawberry Frozen Yogurt Squares...............77
77. Smoked Tofu Quesadillas............................77
78. Zucchini Pizza Boats...................................77
79. Pear-Cranberry Pie with Oatmeal Streusel...................................................................77
80. Macerated Summer Berries with Frozen Yogurt..................................................................78
81. Pumpkin Pie Spiced Yogurt ........................78
82. Maple-Mashed Sweet Potatoes...................78
83. Garlic-Parmesan Cheesy Chips...................78
84. Cheesy Baked Radish Chips.......................79
85. Savory Cheese Biscuits..............................79
86. Italian Herb Muffins....................................79
87. Cheesy Cauliflower Tots.............................80
88. Mozzarella Mushroom Caps........................80
89. Almond-Crusted Mozzarella Sticks..............80
90. Almond Light-As-Air Cookies.......................81
Guided Meditation 8.........................................81

## CHAPTER 13: POULTRY AND MEAT.............86

91. Creamy Chicken Soup and Cauliflower........87
92. Grilled Chicken Wings.................................87
93. Buffalo Chicken Wrap..................................87
94. Chicken Cauliflower Bowls..........................87
95. Chicken Caprese.........................................88
96. Pulled Chicken............................................88
97. Chicken, Barley, and Vegetable Soup............88
98. Ranch-Seasoned Crispy Chicken Tenders..................................................................89
99 a. Healthy Chicken Burgers (Low-Carb & Paleo)...................................................................89
99 b. Grilled Chicken breast............................90
100. Chicken "Nachos" with Sweet Bell Peppers....................................................................90
101. Jerk Chicken with Mango Salsa.................90
Guided Meditation 9.........................................91
102. Chicken Wrap...........................................91
103. Lemony Drumsticks..................................91
104. Stuffed Chicken Breast.............................92
105. Spicy Chicken Wings................................92
106. Pork Sandwiches......................................92
107. Easy Chili Verde.......................................93
108. Beef Crack...............................................93
109. Pork Posole..............................................93
110. Braised Beef Short Ribs...........................94
111. Beef and Peppers.....................................94
112. Fiesta Pork Sandwiches...........................95
113. Fruity Pork Roast.....................................95
114. Crispy Grilled Pork...................................95

115. Chicken with Creamy Mushroom Sauce......96
116. Green Chili Shredded Pork......96
117. Butternut & Pork Stew......97
Guided Meditation 10......97

## CHAPTER 14: FISH AND SEAFOOD............100

118. Tuna Noodle-Less Casserole......101
119. Slow-Roasted Pesto Salmon......101
120. Herb-Crusted Salmon......101
121. Baked Halibut with Tomatoes and White Wine......102
122. Baked Cod with Fennel And Kalamata Olives......102
123. Cucumber Tuna Salad......103
124. Creamy Salmon Salad......103
Trataka......103
125. Baked Dijon Salmon......103
126. Broiled Fish Fillet......104
127. Baked Lemon Tilapia......104
128. Garlic Shrimp......104
129. Chili Garlic Salmon......105
130. Avocado Salmon Salad......105
131. Salmon cakes recipe (salmon patties)......106
132. Shrimp Ceviche......106
Guided Meditation 11......107

## CHAPTER 15: DRESSING, SAUCE, SEASONING............112

133. Baba Ganoush Dip......113
134. Greek Salad Dressing......113
135. Homemade Enchilada Sauce......113
136. Mango Salsa......114
137. Indian Spiced Lentils......114
138. White Cheese Sauce......114
139. Citrus Horseradish Sauce......115
140. Basil Sauce......115
141. Plum Sauce......115
Guided Meditation 12......115

## CHAPTER 16: SWEET AND TREATS............120

142. Chocolate Avocado Pudding......121
143. Frozen Berry Yogurt......121
144. Raspberry Sorbet......121
145. Mixed Berry Popsicles......121
146. Strawberry Yogurt......121
147. Chia Seed Pudding......122
148. Avocado Hummus......122
149. Choco Protein Balls......122
Focused Meditation......123

## CHAPTER 17: IMPORTANCE OF MINDSET IN CONTROLLING THE DISORDER............124

Endure Difficulties without Losing Your Grit......145
Right Mindset Increases Chances of Improvement......145

## CHAPTER 18: HOW TO MANAGE TROUBLESOME SYMPTOMS WITH MEDITATIONS, MINDFULNESS, YOGA, AND EXERCISES ACCORDING TO YOUR PERSONALITY....126

1-EXERCISE: Find small ways to empower yourself......127
2-EXERCISE: Use positive visualization techniques......127

3-EXERCISE: Find an exercise that balances you...
...................................................127
4-EXERCISE: Have a proper diet to control symptoms..................................................127
1-EXERCISE:....................................................128
2-EXERCISE:....................................................128
3-EXERCISE:....................................................128
4-EXERCISE:....................................................128
5-EXERCISE: ...................................................128
6-EXERCISE:....................................................128

**CHAPTER 19: ILLUSTRATION OF YOGA TECHNIQUES, MINDFULNESS, AND CONCEPTS ON HOW TO INCREASE RESILIENCE .........129**

**MEASUREMENT CONVERSION.................131**

**CONCLUSION ................................................132**

# INTRODUCTION

Bariatric surgery helps many people lose weight, but it's not the best option for everyone. Here are some of the benefits and disadvantages of bariatric surgery to help you decide if this is an option for you.

## WHAT IS IT?

Bariatric surgery can reduce stomach size, which in turn helps some people lose weight easier than they could before. People who have obesity that is caused by changes in lifestyle or other risk factors, like diabetes or high cholesterol levels, may benefit from having bariatric surgery, but this isn't always the case...

## WHO WOULD BENEFIT FROM IT?

Most people who undergo bariatric surgery lose weight after three to five years. During that time, they may also see improvements in blood pressure and diabetes levels. All of this raises the question of who would benefit from having bariatric surgery versus other weight loss efforts, like the bariatric diet.

## WHAT ARE LIFESTYLE CHANGES?

In this procedure, your surgeon removes most of the stomach, leaving a small section in the lower portion where it connects to your small intestine. This provides more room for food to pass through to the intestines without being broken down or absorbed into your body. Another procedure used is adjustable gastric banding, which uses an adjustable ring around the top of your stomach. The band adjusts so that it can be tightened or loosened to regulate how much food you ingest.

## HOW EFFECTIVE IT IS?

For most people, losing weight after bariatric surgery is extremely effective. Most people who undergo the surgery can maintain a healthy body weight for many years. However, if you are considering bariatric surgery, make sure you understand that there are potential risks involved.

# CHAPTER 1
# THE BASICS OF THE BARIATRIC DIET

Perhaps you've done all to lose weight, even for the majority of your adult life, and nothing has succeeded. Maybe you've established an emotional attachment to food, which you switch to when you're sad or anxious. Alternatively, you might have suffered from your weight your whole life, and simply now, you need the care, knowledge, and advice that bariatric surgery provides, but weight loss surgery is not a quick fix. Many people think this way, but they don't know that maintaining weight loss requires a lifetime of commitment and healthy choices and that surgery isn't the solution. There's still the question of undergoing major surgery in and of itself. This necessitates a patient's lifestyle and nutrition to be entirely changed both before and after the procedure. Weight loss surgery will give you the confidence and mindset you have to lose more weight to hold it off in the long run. This is since, based on the type of surgery you had, you would be unable to eat or ingest as many calories as you did before surgery. The most famous weight reduction surgical bariatric procedure done in the United States and worldwide is Gastric Sleeve Surgery, commonly known as Vertical Sleeve Gastrectomy. This is a type of weight-loss surgery in which part of the stomach is removed, and the rest is fused to form a sleeve or banana shape. This operation reduces your stomach's scale to around a tenth of its original size, allowing you to consume less and feel full faster. Usually, 60-70% of the stomach is removed. Its normal volume of up to 48 ounces of food is reduced to about 10-15 ounces. This lowers total food intake, makes you feel full quickly, and can help you lose weight. Many people believe that having bariatric surgery is all that is necessary to reduce weight. This is real, but most patients would find themselves back at square one with unhealthy dietary patterns. It is important to develop new eating patterns to live a healthier lifestyle. Tracking your calories in a nutrition plan, changing current recipes for healthier ingredients, or simply following the recipes in this cookbook are both helpful ways to develop and sustain healthy eating habits. So, follow the tips and meal schedule in this book religiously, and you'll be on the way to a safe, healthier lifestyle in no time.

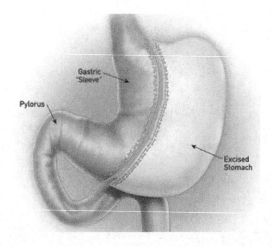

## DIFFERENCE BETWEEN GASTRIC SLEEVE AND GASTRIC BYPASS

By forming a narrow gastric pouch from the upper portion of the stomach, the gastric bypass laparoscopic technique limits food consumption and shortens the digestive tract. The intestine is surgically bound to this pocket, allowing food to flow into a small opening. The remainder of the stomach, as well as a part of the intestines, are bypassed. Gastric bypass surgery decreases the number of calories and nutrients absorbed from food by limiting the amount of food consumed.

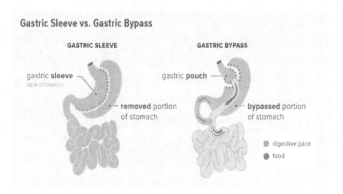

A sleeve gastrectomy involves developing a sleeve-shaped tube from a small part of the stomach and removing the rest of the stomach. Food enters the intestines directly through the new stomach tube. Nutrients and calories are absorbed naturally from food, but patients feel full faster and for longer. Sleeve gastrectomy is a laparoscopic procedure that may be used to permanently manage weight.

## BENEFITS OF GASTRIC SLEEVE BARIATRIC SURGERY

One of the most important reasons for bariatric surgery is severe obesity, although it is not the only one; other prominent reasons include:

- Improved Health. Weight loss surgery typically improves an individual's health and wellbeing.
- Weight loss procedure has been shown to significantly improve fertility conditions. Following substantial weight loss regulates hormones, which improves fertility rates.
- Fewer Hunger Pangs. As 60-75% of your stomach is removed, the Ghrelin hunger hormone's amount is reduced.
- Hauling around excess weight places a lot of strain on the knees, creating pain and damage daily. Individuals

may have greater mobility and a healthy body as a result of their weight loss.

No matter whether you've opted to have a sleeve gastrectomy, pay attention to your diet both before and after the procedure. The first year after the surgery is the most important. You must concentrate on weight management while not reverting to your old eating patterns. You must adhere to a lifestyle that is beneficial to your overall health. And ensure to make the following adjustments:

- Eat right. Eat three regular meals and two snacks every day.
- Drink plenty of water to keep hydrated, and avoid caffeine, alcohol, soda, and juices.
- Get enough rest.
- Set aside at least 40 minutes a week to exercise.
- Take the multivitamins regularly.

# CHAPTER 2
# MENTAL APPROACH TO THE DISORDER, DEVELOPING RESILIENCE

Being able to adjust to life's issues and setbacks is referred to as resilience. Test your level of resiliency and get advice on how to improve it.

When you have resilience, you can draw on inner strength to help you recover from a setback or struggle, especially related to an illness. You may linger on difficulties, feel victimized, become overwhelmed, or resort to unhealthy coping techniques, such as substance misuse if you lack resilience.

Resilience won't make your issues go away, but it can help you see past them, find joy in life, and deal with stress more effectively. If you aren't as resilient as you'd like to be, you can improve your resilience by learning new abilities.

## ADAPTING TO ADVERSITY IS A SKILL THAT MAY BE LEARNED

The ability to adapt to adversity is referred to as resilience. You still feel wrath, grief, and anguish when stress, hardship, or trauma occurs, but you're able to operate – both physically and psychologically. On the other hand, resilience isn't about enduring adversity, being stoic, or sorting things out on your own. One of the most important aspects of resilience is the ability to seek help from others.

## MENTAL HEALTH AND RESILIENCE

Resilience can aid in the prevention of mental illnesses such as sadness and anxiety. The struggles caused by the illness might increase the likelihood of mental health problems. Resilience can help offset these risks and can help you cope better

## TIPS FOR BOOSTING YOUR RESILIENCY

Consider the following suggestions if you want to become more resilient:

- **Establish a connection.** In both good and terrible times, having strong, positive relationships with loved ones and friends may give you much-needed support and acceptance. Volunteering or joining a church or spiritual community can help you make other crucial relationships.
- **Make every day count.** Every day, do something that makes you feel accomplished and purposeful. Make a list of goals to help you look forward to the future with purpose.
- **Learn from your mistakes.** Consider how you've dealt with adversity in the past. Consider the abilities and methods that aided you in overcoming adversity. You may also keep a journal of your past experiences to help you identify positive and negative behavior patterns, as well as to guide your future conduct.
- **Don't lose hope.** You can't undo what is happening, but you can always look forward. Accepting and even anticipating change makes it easier to adjust and cope with new problems.
- **Look after yourself.** Pay attention to your wants and emotions. Participate in hobbies and activities that you enjoy, also considering your current physical status. Make sure you get enough rest. Maintain a balanced diet. Yoga, meditation, guided visualization, deep breathing, and prayer are examples of stress management and relaxation strategies.
- **Take the initiative.** Don't put off dealing with your issues. Instead, determine what needs to be done, devise a strategy and then do it. Although it may take time to recover, keep in mind that your condition will improve if you work hard enough.

# CHAPTER 3
# BARIATRIC LIFESTYLE

## BEFORE THE SURGERY

### HOW DOES GASTRIC SLEEVE SURGERY WORK?

By the time the surgical procedure is complete, the surgeon will have removed approximately 85% of the stomach and reformed it into the shape of a sleeve. To successfully remove the stomach, the surgeon will insert a viewing camera called a laparoscope and other medical instruments through the incisions to remove the stomach. To seal off the remainder of the stomach once the rest of it is removed, the surgeon will seal it off with staples.

Sometimes, gastric sleeve surgery is only the first part of a surgical procedure that will include gastric bypass surgery, which would happen approximately a year (give or take a few months) following the first procedure. However, this is not always necessary. The only advantage to getting gastric bypass surgery done after a gastric sleeve procedure is that the risks of the gastric bypass will be significantly lower.

Another type of surgery that may or may not be required after gastric sleeve surgery is plastic surgery. The reason why plastic surgery may be necessary after a weight-loss operation is because some excess fat and skin could need to be removed to create a better bodily profile. Examples include a body lift or arm lift surgery, both of which are viewed as post-bariatric procedures.

## AFTER THE SURGERY

Gastric sleeve surgery is done under general anesthesia and takes no more than two hours. You should wake up in a hospital room shortly after surgery, where you will be watched for the next few days.

For many days, your abdomen will be painful, but this can be relieved with pain medicine prescribed by your doctor. You'll have scars on your abdomen and stomach as well.

You must focus on altering your diet after the operation.

Over six months, you may anticipate dropping between 50 and 80% of your overall body weight due to the treatment. However, not all of your progress will be due to weight loss. Diabetic control, blood pressure control, and cholesterol control should all improve. The advantages you observe in these areas should be comparable to the advantages you'd get from other weight-loss treatments in the same categories.

Following the surgery, you will need to make certain lifestyle adjustments. This is to ensure that the surgery's advantages will benefit you in the long run. Behavioral modification strategies (for example, learning to eat slowly and chew completely), getting sufficient exercise to maintain your weight, and following precise diet guidelines for the rest of your life are some of the lifestyle adjustments you'll need to make.

## COMPLICATIONS AFTER SURGERY?

One potential risk is that your sleeve could leak. This is because the inside of your stomach will be stapled following the surgery, and if one of the staples fails to hold, it could result in a leak of stomach acids. Since this can infect some of the surrounding tissues, you would be wise to have an operation done to correct the issue.

Because gastric sleeve surgery is a far safer procedure than other weight-loss operations, for instance, your chances of developing wound infections, having any foreign objects left in your body following the procedure, or having nutrients fail to be absorbed are issues that should not be a problem with gastric sleeve surgery. In addition, because there is no gastric band placed in your stomach, there is, therefore, no chance of the band slipping or becoming infected on its own. While gastric sleeve surgery may be a newer form of surgery, it is non-reversible and does not require any adjustments.

## STAGES OF DIET

You should heed the surgical team's instructions to the letter because they are familiar with you, your medical history, and the treatments you've had. They do recommend, however, that you eat in five stages:

- Stage 1: Clear Liquids
- Stage 2: Full Liquids
- Stage 3: Pureed Foods
- Stage 4: Soft Foods
- Stage 5: Eating Well for Life

## FOOD CRAVINGS

You may find that you've lost your appetite, that meals don't thrill you, and that the prospect of eating new foods makes you feel nauseated in the days after surgery. This is completely normal; following surgery, the body experiences fast hormonal and physical changes, and it may take some time for you to revert to your previous self and regain interest in the meals you used to enjoy.

Maintain a strict diet regimen; food can be seen as nothing more than nourishment for the body. You will drop weight quicker than you think if you put a little effort and thought into what you put in your stomach, avoid high-calorie snacks, and adjust pre-existing meals to include nutritious ingredients. Consider your long-term progress.

Following the surgery, you will need to make certain lifestyle adjustments. This is to ensure that the surgery's advantages will benefit you in the long run. Behavioral modification strategies (for example, learning to eat slowly and chew completely), getting sufficient exercise to maintain your weight, and following precise diet guidelines for the rest of your life are some of the lifestyle adjustments you'll need to make.

## FOOD TO EAT AND AVOID AFTER SURGERY

Bariatric surgery causes several changes in a person's physique. It will take time for these alterations to heal and adjust. The typical size of the stomach pouch is decreased to a very small version of its original size once the operation is done. This little stomach will take some time to repair and adjust to the demands of the body. Not only can you eat less, but you also need to eat foods that are readily digestible and do not place undue pressure on your stomach. Furthermore, one must guarantee that the body receives all of the necessary nutrients to live a healthy life.

While the quantity sizes of the meals you may eat and avoid following bariatric surgery will vary depending on the doctor who cares for you, here are some of the things you can eat and avoid:

### THICKER LIQUIDS ONE CAN HAVE:
- Cereals low in fiber
- Soy-based drinks (low in calories)
- Sugar-free natural pudding
- Nonfat yogurt
- Nonfat milk
- Low-fat cheese
- Blended broth
- Lactose-free drinks (low in calories)
- High-protein liquid supplement (low in calories)

### SOFT FOODS:
- Tuna fish
- Mashed potatoes
- Noodles
- Canned fruits
- Applesauce
- Scrambled egg whites
- Lean fish
- Tofu
- Well-cooked vegetables (pureed, if required)
- Lean poultry products

### FOOD TO AVOID AFTER THE SURGERY:

- Oatmeal
- Foods containing fat
- Sugar beverage
- Alcohol
- Red meat
- Spicy food
- Caffeine
- Dry meat
- Carbonated beverages
- All bread

## TYPES OF DIETS

It is a less intrusive procedure with excellent outcomes when compared to other bariatric procedures. In addition to the conventional gastric sleeve, there are various kinds of gastric sleeve, such as strengthened or virtual.

### REINFORCED GASTRIC SLEEVE

During the intervention of the gastric sleeve, the stomach is sectioned, leaving it in the form of a tube or sleeve.

There are three different methods to reinforce the staple line:
- Suture: once in-line stapling is reinforced with a polypropylene suture.
- Absorbable reinforcement material: line reinforcement with biological material such as collagen.
- Fibrin glue: It is applied to the cut line to plug possible leaks.

These reinforcement methods not only prevent possible leaks in the stapling line but also distribute the pressure exerted on the staples when the stomach digests.

### VIRTUAL GASTRIC SLEEVE

The virtual gastric sleeve is a process of stomach reduction through hypnosis. This procedure reprograms the mind to help the patient lose weight in a less invasive way.

It is necessary to complete the treatment, to carry out reinforcement sessions to help the patient cope with the common situations, and have the tools to face them. In addition, it must be completed with a meal plan established by a nutritionist that takes into account the needs of each patient.

A surgical procedure allows regulating appetite, intake, and absorption of food.

According to the type of technique used, it is classified as:

- **Gastric bypass**: The stomach is sectioned, and the proximal intestine is attached, leaving part of it without absorption. It is currently performed laparoscopically and requires a short period of hospitalization.
- **Gastric sleeve**: Vertical section of the stomach that reduces its content, which allows feeding with few amounts without altering intestinal transit.
- **Intragastric balloon:** It consists of the installation of a balloon in the stomach that reduces its space. It is a transitory procedure and is indicated in people who require a small weight loss.

# CHAPTER 4
# LIQUID RECIPES MEAL PREP FOR FIRST 2 WEEKS

# WEEK 1

| Day | Breakfast | Lunch | Dinner |
|---|---|---|---|
| 1 | Sugar-Free Strawberry Limeade | Alcohol-Free Mint Mojito | Hearty Mint Tea |
| 2 | Orange and Apricot Juice | Sugar-Free Strawberry Limeade | Orange and Apricot Juice |
| 3 | Apple and Citrus Juice | Blueberry Cacao Blast | Blueberry Cacao Blast |
| 4 | Blueberry Cacao Blast | Cucumber and Avocado Dill Smoothie | Spinach Green Smoothie |
| 5 | Spinach Green Smoothie | Coco - Banana Milkshake | Coco - Banana Milkshake |
| 6 | Strawberry and Cherry Shake | Banana-Cherry Smoothie | Chia Blueberry Banana Oatmeal Smoothie |
| 7 | Cashew Milk | Pumpkin and carrot soup | Mango Smoothie |

# WEEK 2

| Day | Breakfast | Lunch | Dinner |
|---|---|---|---|
| 1 | Sugar-Free Strawberry Limeade | Alcohol-Free Mint Mojito | Hearty Mint Tea |
| 2 | Orange and Apricot Juice | Sugar-Free Strawberry Limeade | Orange and Apricot Juice |
| 3 | Apple and Citrus Juice | Blueberry Cacao Blast | Blueberry Cacao Blast |
| 4 | Blueberry Cacao Blast | Cucumber and Avocado Dill Smoothie | Spinach Green Smoothie |
| 5 | Spinach Green Smoothie | Coco - Banana Milkshake | Coco - Banana Milkshake |
| 6 | Strawberry and Cherry Shake | Banana-Cherry Smoothie | Chia Blueberry Banana Oatmeal Smoothie |
| 7 | Cashew Milk | Pumpkin and carrot soup | Mango Smoothie |

# CHAPTER 5
# MEAL PREP PUREED AND SOFT RECIPES FOR 4 WEEKS

# WEEK 1

| Day | Breakfast | Lunch | Dinner |
|---|---|---|---|
| 1 | Apple Cinnamon Protein Oatmeal | Apple Parfait | Apple Parfait |
| 2 | Butternut Squash, Cashew and Turkey Puree | Butternut Squash and Turkey Puree | Chicken, Potato and Green Bean Puree |
| 3 | Chocolate Protein Oats | Blueberry Pie Parfait | Chicken Apple Zucchini Puree |
| 4 | Chocolate Parfait | Chocolate Parfait | Scrambled Eggs with Black Bean Puree |
| 5 | Frozen Mocha Frappuccino | Oatmeal Cookie Shake | Black Bean and Lime Puree |
| 6 | Pumpkin Protein Smoothie | Apple Cucumber Juice | Chocolate PB2 Banana Protein Shake |
| 7 | Vitamin C Juice | Coco-Rita Cocktail | Cherry Mango Smoothie |

# WEEK 2

| Day | Breakfast | Lunch | Dinner |
|---|---|---|---|
| 1 | Apple Cinnamon Protein Oatmeal | Apple Parfait | Apple Parfait |
| 2 | Butternut Squash, Cashew and Turkey Puree | Butternut Squash and Turkey Puree | Chicken, Potato and Green Bean Puree |
| 3 | Chocolate Protein Oats | Blueberry Pie Parfait | Chicken Apple Zucchini Puree |
| 4 | Chocolate Parfait | Chocolate Parfait | Scrambled Eggs with Black Bean Puree |
| 5 | Frozen Mocha Frappuccino | Oatmeal Cookie Shake | Black Bean and Lime Puree |
| 6 | Pumpkin Protein Smoothie | Apple Cucumber Juice | Chocolate PB2 Banana Protein Shake |
| 7 | Vitamin C Juice | Coco-Rita Cocktail | Cherry Mango Smoothie |

# WEEK 3

| Day | Breakfast | Lunch | Dinner |
|---|---|---|---|
| 1 | Apple Cinnamon Protein Oatmeal | Apple Parfait | Apple Parfait |
| 2 | Butternut Squash, Cashew and Turkey Puree | Butternut Squash and Turkey Puree | Chicken, Potato and Green Bean Puree |
| 3 | Chocolate Protein Oats | Blueberry Pie Parfait | Chicken Apple Zucchini Puree |
| 4 | Chocolate Parfait | Chocolate Parfait | Scrambled Eggs with Black Bean Puree |
| 5 | Frozen Mocha Frappuccino | Oatmeal Cookie Shake | Black Bean and Lime Puree |
| 6 | Pumpkin Protein Smoothie | Apple Cucumber Juice | Chocolate PB2 Banana Protein Shake |
| 7 | Vitamin C Juice | Coco-Rita Cocktail | Cherry Mango Smoothie |

# WEEK 4

| Day | Breakfast | Lunch | Dinner |
|---|---|---|---|
| 1 | Apple Cinnamon Protein Oatmeal | Apple Parfait | Apple Parfait |
| 2 | Butternut Squash, Cashew and Turkey Puree | Butternut Squash and Turkey Puree | Chicken, Potato and Green Bean Puree |
| 3 | Chocolate Protein Oats | Blueberry Pie Parfait | Chicken Apple Zucchini Puree |
| 4 | Chocolate Parfait | Chocolate Parfait | Scrambled Eggs with Black Bean Puree |
| 5 | Frozen Mocha Frappuccino | Oatmeal Cookie Shake | Black Bean and Lime Puree |
| 6 | Pumpkin Protein Smoothie | Apple Cucumber Juice | Chocolate PB2 Banana Protein Shake |
| 7 | Vitamin C Juice | Coco-Rita Cocktail | Cherry Mango Smoothie |

# CHAPTER 6
# FOOD PRE AND GENERAL DIET FOR 6 WEEKS

# WEEK 1

| Day | Breakfast | Lunch | Dinner |
|---|---|---|---|
| 1 | Pumpkin protein pancakes | Chicken Cauliflower Bowls | Creamy Chicken Soup and Cauliflower |
| 2 | Mocha banana protein smoothie bowl | Ranch-Seasoned Crispy Chicken Tenders | Chicken, Barley, and Vegetable Soup |
| 3 | Blackberry vanilla French toast | Beef Crack | Spicy Chicken Wings |
| 4 | Apple and goat cheese sandwich | Fruity Pork Roast | Green Chili Shredded Pork |
| 5 | Easy Baked Salmon | Slow-Roasted Pesto Salmon | Baked Dijon Salmon |
| 6 | Quinoa Bowls | Cucumber Tuna Salad | Avocado Salmon Salad |
| 7 | Asparagus Omelet | Garlic Shrimp | Shrimp Ceviche |

# WEEK 2

| Day | Breakfast | Lunch | Dinner |
|---|---|---|---|
| 1 | Pumpkin protein pancakes | Chicken Cauliflower Bowls | Creamy Chicken Soup and Cauliflower |
| 2 | Mocha banana protein smoothie bowl | Ranch-Seasoned Crispy Chicken Tenders | Chicken, Barley, and Vegetable Soup |
| 3 | Blackberry vanilla French toast | Beef Crack | Spicy Chicken Wings |
| 4 | Apple and goat cheese sandwich | Fruity Pork Roast | Green Chili Shredded Pork |
| 5 | Easy Baked Salmon | Slow-Roasted Pesto Salmon | Baked Dijon Salmon |
| 6 | Quinoa Bowls | Cucumber Tuna Salad | Avocado Salmon Salad |
| 7 | Asparagus Omelet | Garlic Shrimp | Shrimp Ceviche |

# WEEK 3

| Day | Breakfast | Lunch | Dinner |
|---|---|---|---|
| 1 | Pumpkin protein pancakes | Chicken Cauliflower Bowls | Creamy Chicken Soup and Cauliflower |
| 2 | Mocha banana protein smoothie bowl | Ranch-Seasoned Crispy Chicken Tenders | Chicken, Barley, and Vegetable Soup |
| 3 | Blackberry vanilla French toast | Beef Crack | Spicy Chicken Wings |
| 4 | Apple and goat cheese sandwich | Fruity Pork Roast | Green Chili Shredded Pork |
| 5 | Easy Baked Salmon | Slow-Roasted Pesto Salmon | Baked Dijon Salmon |
| 6 | Quinoa Bowls | Cucumber Tuna Salad | Avocado Salmon Salad |
| 7 | Asparagus Omelet | Garlic Shrimp | Shrimp Ceviche |

# WEEK 4

| Day | Breakfast | Lunch | Dinner |
|---|---|---|---|
| 1 | Pumpkin protein pancakes | Chicken Cauliflower Bowls | Creamy Chicken Soup and Cauliflower |
| 2 | Mocha banana protein smoothie bowl | Ranch-Seasoned Crispy Chicken Tenders | Chicken, Barley, and Vegetable Soup |
| 3 | Blackberry vanilla French toast | Beef Crack | Spicy Chicken Wings |
| 4 | Apple and goat cheese sandwich | Fruity Pork Roast | Green Chili Shredded Pork |
| 5 | Easy Baked Salmon | Slow-Roasted Pesto Salmon | Baked Dijon Salmon |
| 6 | Quinoa Bowls | Cucumber Tuna Salad | Avocado Salmon Salad |
| 7 | Asparagus Omelet | Garlic Shrimp | Shrimp Ceviche |

# WEEK 5

| Day | Breakfast | Lunch | Dinner |
|---|---|---|---|
| 1 | Pumpkin protein pancakes | Chicken Cauliflower Bowls | Creamy Chicken Soup and Cauliflower |
| 2 | Mocha banana protein smoothie bowl | Ranch-Seasoned Crispy Chicken Tenders | Chicken, Barley, and Vegetable Soup |
| 3 | Blackberry vanilla French toast | Beef Crack | Spicy Chicken Wings |
| 4 | Apple and goat cheese sandwich | Fruity Pork Roast | Green Chili Shredded Pork |
| 5 | Easy Baked Salmon | Slow-Roasted Pesto Salmon | Baked Dijon Salmon |
| 6 | Quinoa Bowls | Cucumber Tuna Salad | Avocado Salmon Salad |
| 7 | Asparagus Omelet | Garlic Shrimp | Shrimp Ceviche |

# WEEK 6

| Day | Breakfast | Lunch | Dinner |
|---|---|---|---|
| 1 | Pumpkin protein pancakes | Chicken Cauliflower Bowls | Creamy Chicken Soup and Cauliflower |
| 2 | Mocha banana protein smoothie bowl | Ranch-Seasoned Crispy Chicken Tenders | Chicken, Barley, and Vegetable Soup |
| 3 | Blackberry vanilla French toast | Beef Crack | Spicy Chicken Wings |
| 4 | Apple and goat cheese sandwich | Fruity Pork Roast | Green Chili Shredded Pork |
| 5 | Easy Baked Salmon | Slow-Roasted Pesto Salmon | Baked Dijon Salmon |
| 6 | Quinoa Bowls | Cucumber Tuna Salad | Avocado Salmon Salad |
| 7 | Asparagus Omelet | Garlic Shrimp | Shrimp Ceviche |

# CHAPTER 7
# EMOTIONAL RESILIENCE AND MEDITATION EXERCISES

The key to developing emotional resilience and well-being is to concentrate on the things you can control.

The barriers between family, career, and oneself have blurred for parents. Making time for mental wellness is extremely crucial for them. Self-care is not an afterthought, but something planned out, even if it's only for two or five minutes a day, she continues. It's critical to show your children how to do this.

## PACED BREATHING CAN HELP YOU DEAL WITH ANXIETY

- Take a minute every day to concentrate on your breathing. Here's how to do it:
- Inhale deeply through your nose and exhale deeply through your mouth.
- Slowly and deeply inhale until your lungs are fully inflated.
- Exhale slowly until your lungs are empty.
- Deep breathing offers short-term and long-term benefits in reducing stress and anxiety.

## AVOID FALLING INTO "THINKING TRAPS"

In times of uncertainty, it's crucial to reflect on our thoughts. Learning the talent will benefit you for the rest of your life.

- **Thinking in black-and-white terms:** Assuming that everything is either perfect or amazing, or that everything is horrible.
- **Catastrophic thinking:** This is when you expect the worst possible event and believe you won't be able to cope if it happens.
- **Predicting the future:** Assuming you know what will happen in the future (for example, "I won't be able to go back to school, I'll never receive the degree I require, and I won't attend college").

## HOW TO STAY OUT OF THESE SNARES:

- **Catch yourself:** Recognize when you're about to fall into a trap. You may begin to feel depressed, anxious, or hopeless.
- **Think more realistically or holistically:** Ask yourself, or discuss with a trusted friend or family member, what is real and what isn't really about your views. Where are the ambiguous areas? Are you overlooking more feasible "in-between" possibilities?
- **Create a coping mantra:** Think of a phrase that will help you respond to your problems. "I'm doing the best I can, and I'll be fine," you could say.

Being able to control the intensity of our emotions can lead to more self-care and more effective behavior for our mental health.

## MAINTAIN A GRATITUDE NOTEBOOK

A thankfulness habit can help even little children. Make a list of three things you loved and were grateful for in a notepad or journal during the day. It could be something as simple as a tasty snack, quality time with a pet, or something you witnessed outside.

"Think of a silver lining for the day," says the narrator. "How we feel can be affected by that adjustment in thinking. It can assist us in managing our emotions and the actions we take in response."

## PARTICIPATE IN BEHAVIORAL ACTIVATION EXERCISES

"Being behaviorally stimulated gives our moods a boost." Physical activity, such as exercise, can be considered behavioral activation. However, any activity that gives you a sensation of control and action might be included. You could try the following activation methods:

Physical activation includes things like exercise, dancing, deep breathing, and relaxing your muscles. Try these five bone-strengthening exercises for people who have Gaucher disease.

- **Thoughts and feelings:** Activation can be achieved through creative undertakings such as painting, drawing, or even jigsaw puzzles. Outward-focused activities, such as a service project that benefits others, can also be beneficial.
- **Mastery:** Developing a new skill might provide you with a sense of accomplishment. You may utilize this time to practice your instrument or study a language with an app.
- **Sensory:** You may make a self-soothing kit to assist you to calm down and ground yourself when you're feeling anxious. Include something to appeal to each of your five senses: something aesthetically appealing, a pleasant odor, and tactile, auditory, and gustatory experiences.

When we're upset or experiencing strong emotions, we typically feel compelled to withdraw. The desire to avoid things is a common symptom of anxiety. However, from a behavioral standpoint, it may be beneficial to consider the opposite action—interacting with others and being interested." "We may take little measures to confront fear safely.

For example, coronavirus may make you nervous about going to a doctor's appointment. Make an informed decision by assessing the risks and advantages. Wear a mask, wash your hands, and maintain social space to help you center yourself and realize you're fine.

## KEEP TRACK OF HOW MUCH TIME YOU SPEND ON YOUR DEVICE AND HOW MUCH NEWS YOU CONSUME

It might be difficult to stay informed in today's always-on society without becoming overwhelmed. Adults, teens, and children are all affected by the availability of smartphones, tablets, and a continual stream of information.

Before COVID, studies revealed that excessive usage of electronics can raise anxiety and depression in youth who are predisposed to feeling anxious and depressed. However, during the pandemic, social media served as a method for teens and tweens to stay in touch.

"The trick is to strike a healthy balance between socializing with friends and getting work done. It shouldn't be about the number of likes on an Instagram photo or the fear of losing out." "For parents, that means keeping the lines of communication open about what makes sense for their family and what's best for them."

Adults find it difficult to spend so much time in front of a screen. Zoom fatigue and screen weariness are both real. It's a terrific time to get creative with doing things outside as a family now that school is out and the weather is getting nicer. During this time, we all need technology to stay connected.

But, whether it's writing letters or going for bike rides, balance your device time with old-school means of having fun and pleasure.

"It's fine to interact with pals through social media or gaming, and it's also fine to set a limit."

# CHAPTER 8
## LIQUID RECIPES

BE PART OF THIS COMMUNITY OF CRAZY INNOVATORS AND SHARE YOUR
UNCONVENTIONAL KNOWLEDGE...BE PART OF ...
FUN CLUB KITCHEN

## 1. ALCOHOL-FREE MINT MOJITO

**Preparation Time:** 5 minutes
**Cooking Time:** 30 minutes
**Servings:** 4
**Ingredients for 1 person:**
- 12/2 cup fresh mint leaves
- 1 oz. lime juice
- ½ cup natural sweetener
- 2 cups water

**Directions:**
1. Add water and sweetener to a pot and let it boil for 5 minutes until the syrup has thickened.
2. Transfer mint leaves to a glass jar and pour in the syrup.
3. Cover the jar and let it steep for 20 minutes.
4. Create a mixture of a tablespoon of syrup and half a cup of cold water in a glass, add lime juice, mix, serve and enjoy!

**Nutrition:**
Calories: 32, Total Fat: 0 g, Saturated Fat: 0 g, Protein: 0 g, Carbs: 3 g, Fiber: 1 g

## 2. SUGAR-FREE STRAWBERRY LIMEADE

**Preparation Time:** 5 minutes
**Cooking Time:** 30 minutes
**Servings:** 4
**Ingredients for 1 person:**
- ½ teaspoon strawberry extract
- 1 and ½ cup cold water
- ½ a lime juice

**Directions:**
1. Mix in strawberry extract, lime juice, and water in a bowl.
2. Take a cup and add ice cubes, pour the strawberry mixture and enjoy!

**Nutrition:**
Calories: 12, Total Fat: 0 g, Saturated Fat: 0 g, Protein: 1 g, Carbs: 2.1 g, Fiber: 0.5 g

## 3. HEARTY MINT TEA

**Preparation Time:** 5 minutes
**Cooking Time:** 30 minutes
**Servings:** 4
**Ingredients for 1 person:**
- 1 gallon boiling water
- 2 tablespoons mint
- 1 lemon, sliced
- 6 Rooibos tea bags

**Directions:**
1. Place water over high heat and let it start boiling.
2. Remove heat and add tea bags.
3. Pour the mixture into a pitcher (alongside tea bags, mint, and sliced lemon) and let it steep for 30 minutes.
4. Serve and enjoy!

**Nutrition:**
Calories: 4, Total Fat: 0 g, Saturated Fat: 0 g, Protein: 0.1 g, Carbs: 1.4 g, Fiber: 0.1 g

## 4. ORANGE AND APRICOT JUICE

**Preparation Time:** 10 minutes
**Cooking Time:** nil
**Servings:** 2
**Ingredients for 1 person:**
- 2 large oranges, peeled
- 2 large apricots, pitted
- 1 cup pomegranate seeds
- 1 cup green grapes
- 1 large lemon, peeled
- 1 small ginger slice, peeled

**Directions:**
1. Peel oranges and divide them into wedges.
2. Keep it on the side.
3. Wash apricots and cut them in half, remove pits, and cut them into small pieces.
4. Cut the top of the pomegranate fruit using a sharp knife and slice down each of the white membranes inside the fruit.
5. Pop seeds into a measuring cup and keep it on the side.
6. Peel the lemon, cut it lengthwise in half, and keep it on the side.
7. Peel ginger slices and keep them on the side.
8. Add orange, apricots, pomegranate, lemon and ginger to a juicer and process until well juiced.
9. Chill for 20 minutes and enjoy!

**Nutrition:**
Calories: 196, Total Fat: 0.8 g, Saturated Fat: 0 g, Protein: 4 g, Carbs: 48 g, Fiber: 6.9 g

## 5. GINGER AND LIME JUICE

**Preparation Time:** 10 minutes
**Cooking Time:** nil
**Servings:** 2
**Ingredients for 1 person:**
- 1 cup avocado, pitted and chopped
- 1 large cucumber, sliced
- 1 large lemon, peeled
- 1 cup fresh spinach, torn
- 1 large lime, peeled
- 1 small ginger knob, peeled
- 3 oz. water

**Directions:**
1. Peel your avocado and cut it in half. Remove the pit and chop the avocado into chunks.
2. Wash the cucumber and cut it into thick slices.
3. Keep it on the side.
4. Peel lemon and lime, cut it length in half.
5. Wash your spinach thoroughly and tear it into small parts.
6. Take your juicer and add avocado, cucumber, lemon, lime, spinach, ginger, and process until finely juiced.
7. Let it chill for 20 minutes, serve and enjoy!

**Nutrition:**
Calories: 197, Total Fat: 14 g, Saturated Fat: 3 g, Protein: 3 g, Carbs: 19 g, Fiber: 8 g

## 6. BLUEBERRY CACAO BLAST

**Preparation Time:** 2 minutes
**Cooking Time:** 3 minutes
**Servings:** 1
**Ingredients for 1 person:**
- 1 cup blueberries
- 1 tablespoon raw cacao nibs
- 1 tablespoon chia seeds
- 1 dash cinnamon
- ½ cup chopped spinach
- ½ cup chopped bananas
- 1½ cup almond milk
- 2 scoops whey protein powder

**Directions:**
1. Place raspberries, cacao nibs, chia seeds, and cinnamon in a blender.
2. Add enough almond milk to reach the max line.
3. Process for 30 seconds or until you get a smooth mixture.
4. Serve immediately in a tall chilled glass.

**Nutrition:**
Calories: 321, Carbs: 69.4 g, Fat: 2.7 g, Protein: 24.7 g

## 7. CUCUMBER AND AVOCADO DILL SMOOTHIE

**Preparation Time:** 2 minutes
**Cooking Time:** 3 minutes
**Servings:** 2
**Ingredients for 1 person:**
- 1 sliced cucumber
- 2 tablespoons chopped dill
- 2 tablespoons lemon juice
- 1 pitted avocado
- 1 cup coconut milk
- 1 teaspoon shredded coconut
- 2 sliced kiwi fruit

**Directions:**
1. Mix and blend all the above ingredients using a blender.
2. Drain the extract and discard residue.
3. Serve and enjoy.

**Nutrition:**
Calories: 165, Fat: 5.5 g, Carbs: 24.8 g, Protein: 2.3 g

## GUIDED MEDITATION 1

Start by finding a place that is relaxed and comfortable and with no possibility of disturbances. Sit and make sure your back is straight, breathe using your nose, and exhale through your mouth. Inhale and exhale in this particular for at least 5 to 10 minutes or more and relax your body as you do this. Imagine drawing up green energy towards your heart via your body, starting at the base of your body and up to your heart and out. Imagine that green energy becoming brighter and bigger as you inhale and exhale and picture it as a bright huge green ball.

Focus yourself tuning on giving love and compassion to yourself and others while allowing the green energy to radiate through your body and focus on performing these meditation techniques for at least 5 minutes or more.

## 8. SPINACH GREEN SMOOTHIE

Preparation Time:
Cooking Time:
Servings: 2
Ingredients for 1 person:
- 1 cup baby spinach leaves
- 3 mint leave
- 1 cup 100% grapes juice
- 1 cup 100% pineapple juice
- 2 tablespoons lime juice
- 2 scoops protein powder

Directions:
1. In a blender, add ingredients and blend well until puree.
2. Transfer to serving glasses.
3. Serve and enjoy.

Nutrition:
Calories: 268, Fat: 5.5 g, Carbs: 11.4 g, Protein: 24.3 g

## 9. COCO-BANANA MILKSHAKE
by Paul Rader – Ocala

Preparation Time: 2 Minutes
Cooking Time: 3 Minutes
Servings: 1
Ingredients for 1 person:
- 1 cup coconut milk
- 2 ripe bananas
- 2 tablespoons cinnamon
- ¼ tsp. cardamom powder
- 2 scoops protein powder
- Ice cubes

Directions:
1. In a blender, add coconut milk with cardamom powder, cinnamon, bananas, and blend well.
2. Pour into a glass and add ice chunks.
3. Serve and enjoy.

Nutrition:
Calories: 191.9, Fat: 7.1 g, Carbs: 35.8 g, Protein: 25.7 g

## 10. STRAWBERRY AND CHERRY SHAKE
by Edmund Lent – Santa Barbara

Preparation Time: 2 minutes
Cooking Time: 3 minutes
Servings: 2
Ingredients for 1 person:
- 1 cup strawberries
- 1 cup cherries
- 1 cup almond milk
- ½ cup coconut milk
- 2 scoops protein powder
- A few ice chunks

Directions:
1. Place all the ingredients in a blender and process well.
2. Serve and enjoy.

Nutrition:
Calories: 138, Fat: 0 g, Carbs: 30 g, Protein: 20 g

## 11. CHIA BLUEBERRY BANANA OATMEAL
by Patricia Jeffery – Cincinnati

Preparation Time: 3 minutes
Cooking Time: 7 minutes
Servings: 1
Ingredients for 1 person:
- 1 cup soy milk
- 1 sliced frozen banana
- ¼ cup frozen blueberries
- ¼ cup oats
- 1 teaspoon vanilla extract
- 1 teaspoon cinnamon
- 1 tablespoon chia seed

Directions:
1. Use a blender to mix and blend until the ingredients are combined and smooth.
2. Serve and enjoy!

Nutrition:
Calories: 178, Fat: 4.2 g, Carbs: 36.2 g, Protein: 3.2 g

## 12. BANANA-CHERRY SMOOTHIE
by Lynn Harter – Bound Brook

Preparation Time: 2 minutes

**Cooking Time:** 3 minutes
**Servings:** 1

### Ingredients for 1 person:
- 1 banana
- 1 cup pitted cherries
- ¼ teaspoon nutmeg
- 1 scoop protein powder
- 1 cup almond milk

### Directions:
1. Place all ingredients in a blender.
2. Process ingredients until smooth, for 20 seconds.
3. Serve immediately.

**Nutrition:**
Calories: 398, Fat: 2 g, Carbs: 89.2 g, Protein: 17 g

## 13. MANGO SMOOTHIE
by Virginia Grant – Milwaukee

**Preparation Time:** 2 minutes
**Cooking Time:** 3 minutes
**Servings:** 2

### Ingredients for 1 person:
- 2 mangos (seeded, diced, frozen)
- 1 cup milk
- ½ cup crushed ice
- 1 cup plain yogurt
- 2 scoops protein powder

### Directions:
1. Combine all ingredients.
2. Process for 30 seconds or until smooth.
3. Serve immediately in a tall glass.

**Nutrition:**
Calories: 320, Fat: 0 g, Carbs: 8 g, Protein: 21 g

## 14. CASHEW MILK
by Merle Secor – Lombard

**Preparation Time:** 2 minutes
**Cooking Time:** 3 minutes
**Servings:** 5

### Ingredients for 1 person:
- 1 cup cashew, soaked
- 4 cups water
- 3 dates

### Directions:
1. Add all ingredients.
2. Pulse until creamy (should take about 1 min).
3. Enjoy!

**Nutrition:**
Calories: 60, Fat: 2.5 g, Carbs: 27.3 g, Protein: 8 g

## 15. PUMPKIN AND CARROT SOUP
by Matthew Marquis Appleton

**Preparation Time:** 3 minutes
**Cooking Time:** 22 minutes
**Servings:** 4

### Ingredients for 1 person:
- ½ lb. pumpkin puree
- ½ lb. cubed carrots
- 2 cups vegetable stock
- ½ cup chopped onion
- Salt
- Pepper
- 1 teaspoon dried thyme
- 2 oz. cauliflower florets
- ½ tablespoon olive oil
- 1 anise star

### Directions:
1. Heat the oil in a pot. Add onion, cauliflower, and carrots, and sauté for 15 minutes or until the onion is caramelized.
2. Add thyme and stir well.
3. Transfer the vegetables into a Nutri Bullet, add pumpkin puree and vegetable stock, and pulse until smooth.
4. Transfer the mixture into a saucepan and simmer, add anise star and simmer over medium-high heat for 5-8 minutes or until heated through.
5. Remove the anise star and discard it.
6. Strain and serve immediately.

**Nutrition:**
Calories: 70, Fat: 0 g, Carbs: 0 g, Protein: 2 g

## GUIDED MEDITATION 2

Start by closing your eyes or leave them open and inhale deeply and exhale smoothly while uttering the following unifying phrases.

- "I allow accepting everything the way it is at this moment."
- "I am conscious and aware of everything around me."
- "I choose peace."
- "I am at peace with my creator."

Whenever thoughts and pain arise, simply be aware of them and notice them without wishing for another experience or trying to push the experience away. Think of this experience as a passing cloud understanding that everything is impermanent.

You find yourself feeling lighter by the moment, releasing everything that no longer serves and embracing the expansive wisdom that continually surrounds you, allowing the regenerative nature of the universe to become part of you through breath and rhythm. Through the simple act of breathing. This communion with life all around you. And it feels so good to be part of this rhythm.

Notice also how your body becomes more grounded, more connected to the substrate beneath it, to the earth itself. How you are at once light as air and part of the earth. How you are right where you need to be, in the most perfect place for you right now in this entire universe, supported and free.

# PERSONAL NOTES

# PERSONAL NOTES

# CHAPTER 9
# PUREED AND SOFT RECIPES

BE PART OF THIS COMMUNITY OF CRAZY INNOVATORS AND SHARE YOUR UNCONVENTIONAL KNOWLEDGE...BE PART OF ...
FUN CLUB KITCHEN

## 16. HEALTHY CAULIFLOWER BITES

**Preparation Time:** 10 minutes
**Cooking Time:** 15 minutes
**Servings:** 5
**Ingredients for 1 person:**

- 8 oz. cauliflower
- 6 tablespoons almond flour
- 1 teaspoon chili pepper
- 1 teaspoon cayenne pepper
- 1 teaspoon finely ground black pepper
- 1 tomato
- 1 teaspoon diced garlic
- ½ teaspoon salt
- 1 teaspoon extra virgin olive oil

Directions:
1. Wash the cauliflower carefully and separate it into medium florets.
2. Coat the cauliflower florets with salt.
3. Then, cleave the tomato roughly and move it to the blender.
4. Blend it well.
5. Then add the chili pepper, cayenne pepper, finely ground black pepper, and diced garlic.
6. Blend the mixture.
7. Then, heat the air fryer to 350ºF.
8. Coat the air fryer basket with the extra virgin olive oil inside.
9. Coat the cauliflower florets with the blended tomato mixture generously.
10. Then, coat the cauliflower florets in almond flour.
11. Place the coated cauliflower florets in the air fryer basket and cook the dish for 15 minutes.
12. Shake the cauliflower florets every 4 minutes.
13. When the cauliflower is prepared—it will have a light brown color.
14. Move it to the serving plates.
15. Enjoy!

**Nutrition:**
Calories 217, Fat 17.9, Fiber 5.1, Carbs 10.8, Protein 8.4

## 17. BACON CHEDDAR DEVILED EGGS

**Preparation Time:** 10 minutes
**Cooking Time:** 12 minutes
**Servings:** 2
**Ingredients for 1 person:**

- 2 eggs
- 4 oz. bacon
- ¼ teaspoon salt
- ½ teaspoon butter
- 3 oz. Cheddar cheese, minced
- ½ teaspoon cayenne pepper
- ½ teaspoon paprika to taste
- 1 tablespoon chives

Directions:
1. Cut the bacon into tiny pieces and coat it with salt, cayenne pepper, and paprika to taste and mix it well.
2. Then, spread the ramekins with the butter and beat the eggs there. Then add the minced cheese and chives.
3. Then, place the bacon over the chives.
4. Cook the breakfast for 12 minutes.
5. Remove the bacon egg cups from the ramekins carefully.
6. Enjoy!

Nutrition:
Calories 553, Fat 43.3, Fiber 0.4, Carbs 2.3, Protein 37.3

## 18. BUTTERED EGGS WITH STEVIA

**Preparation Time:** 8 minutes
**Cooking Time:** 4 minutes
**Servings:** 2
**Ingredients for 1 person:**

- 2 eggs
- 1 teaspoon butter

**Directions:**
1. Separate the eggs into the egg whites and the egg yolks and then whisk the egg whites with the help of the hand mixer until you get strong white peaks.
2. Then spread the Air Fryer tray with the butter.
3. Heat the Air Fryer to 300ºF.
4. Then, remove the basket from the Air Fryer, place the egg yolks in the center of each egg cloud, and return the basket to the Air Fryer.

5. Cook the dish for 2 minutes more. Serve immediately and Enjoy!

**Nutrition:**
Calories 80, Fat 6.3, Fiber 0, Carbs 0.3, Protein 5.

## 19. BLACKBERRY MUFFINS
*by Arthur Lyall Pierre – Part*

**Preparation Time:** 15 minutes
**Cooking Time:** 10 minutes
**Servings:** 5

**Ingredients for 1 person:**
- 1 teaspoon apple cider vinegar
- 1 cup almond flour
- 4 tablespoon butter
- 6 tablespoons almond milk
- 1 teaspoon baking soda
- 3 oz. blackberry
- ½ teaspoon salt
- 3 teaspoon stevia
- 1 teaspoon vanilla extract

**Directions:**
1. Place the almond flour in the small mixing bowl.
2. Add the baking soda, salt, stevia, and vanilla extract.
3. Then add butter, almond milk, and apple cider vinegar.
4. Smash the blackberries gently and add them to the almond flour mixture.
5. Slowly stir it carefully with the help of the fork until the mass is homogeneous.
6. Then, leave the muffin mixture for 5 minutes in a warm place.
7. Heat the air fryer to 400°F.
8. Prepare the muffin forms.
9. Pour the dough into the muffin forms. Fill only ½ part of each muffin form.
10. When the air fryer is heated – place the muffing forms with the filling in the air fryer basket. Close the air fryer.
11. Cook the muffins for 10 minutes.
12. After the due time—remove the muffins from the air fryer basket.
13. Chill them until they are warm.
14. Serve them and enjoy!

**Nutrition:**
Calories 165, Fat 16.4, Fiber 1.9, Carbs 4, Protein 2

## 20. PAN-FRIED TOFU WITH EGG AND CHIVE
*by Alma Ledesma – Orange City*

**Preparation Time:** 15 minutes
**Cooking Time:** 20 minutes
**Servings:** 5

**Ingredients for 1 person:**
- 10 oz. Tofu cheese
- 2 eggs
- 1 teaspoon chives
- 1 tablespoon apple cider vinegar
- ½ teaspoon salt
- 1 teaspoon finely ground white pepper
- ¼ teaspoon finely ground coriander

**Directions:**
1. Shred tofu cheese and coat it with apple cider vinegar, salt, finely ground white pepper, and finely ground coriander.
2. Then, Heat the air fryer to 370°F.
3. Then, move the marinated minced tofu cheese to the air fryer tray and cook the cheese for 13 minutes.
4. Then, beat the eggs in the small bowl and whisk them.
5. After the due time – pour the egg mixture in the minced tofu cheese and slowly stir it with the help of the spatula well.
6. When the eggs start to be cooked – place the air fryer tray in the air fryer and cook the dish for 7 minutes more.
7. Then, remove the cooked meal from the air fryer tray and serve it.
8. Enjoy!

**Nutrition:**
Calories 109, Fat 6.7, Fiber 1.4, Carbs 2.9, Protein 11.2

*Pureed and Soft Recipes* | 43

## 21. ROASTED CAULIFLOWER FRITTERS
by Lecia Gonzalez – Baltimore

**Preparation Time:** 10 minutes
**Cooking Time:** 15 minutes
**Servings:** 4

**Ingredients for 1 person:**
- 1 tablespoon dried dill
- 1 egg
- 1 teaspoon salt
- 10 oz. cauliflower
- 1 tablespoon almond flour
- 1 teaspoon extra virgin olive oil
- 1 tablespoon parsley
- ½ teaspoon finely ground white pepper

**Directions:**
1. Wash the cauliflower carefully and cut it into small pieces.
2. Then place the cauliflower in the blender and blend it well. Add egg and blend it for 1 minute.
3. Then move the blended cauliflower mixture to the small bowl.
4. Coat it with salt, dried dill, almond flour, parsley, and finely ground white pepper.
5. Mix it well carefully with the help of the spoon.
6. Heat the air fryer to 355ºF.
7. Then coat the air fryer tray with extra virgin olive oil.
8. Make the fritters from the cauliflower mixture and place them in the air fryer tray.
9. Close the air fryer and cook the fritters for 8 minutes.
10. Then, turn the fritters to another side and cook them for 7 minutes more.
11. When the fritters are cooked – serve them hot!
12. Enjoy!

**Nutrition:**
Calories 54, Fat 3.1, Fiber 2.1, Carbs 4.8, Protein 3.3

## 22. SPICY GROUND BEEF ROLLS

**Preparation Time:** 15 minutes
**Cooking Time:** 8 minutes
**Servings:** 6

**Ingredients for 1 person:**
- ½ cup almond flour
- ¼ cup water
- 1 teaspoon salt
- 1 egg
- 7 oz. finely ground beef
- 1 teaspoon paprika, to taste
- 1 teaspoon finely ground black pepper
- 1 tablespoon extra-virgin olive oil

**Directions:**
1. Mix the almond flour with the salt and slowly stir it.
2. Add the boiling water and whisk it carefully until the mixture is homogenous.
3. Then knead the smooth and soft dough.
4. Leave the dough.
5. Then, mix the finely ground beef with the paprika to taste and finely ground black pepper.
6. Mix the mixture well and move it to the pan.
7. Roast the meat mixture for 5 minutes on medium heat. Slowly stir it frequently.
8. Then beat the egg in the meat mixture and scramble it.
9. Cook the finely ground beef mixture for 4 minutes more.
10. Then roll the dough and cut it into 6 squares.
11. Place the finely ground beef mixture in each square.
12. Roll the squares to make the dough sticks.
13. Coat the dough sticks with extra virgin olive oil.
14. Then, place the prepared dough sticks in the air fryer basket.
15. Heat the air fryer to 350ºF and place the egg-meat rolls there.
16. Cook the dish for 8 minutes.
17. When the egg-meat rolls are cooked – move them directly to the serving plates. Enjoy!

**Nutrition:**
Calories 150, Fat 9.6, Fiber 1.2, Carbs 2.5, Protein 13

## 23. CHEESY BACON

**Preparation Time:** 8 minutes
**Cooking Time:** 10 minutes
**Servings:** 4

**Ingredients for 1 person:**
- 8 oz. bacon

- ½ teaspoon dried oregano
- ½ teaspoon salt
- ½ teaspoon finely ground black pepper
- ½ teaspoon finely ground thyme
- 4 oz. Cheddar cheese

Directions:

1. Put the bacon and rub it with the dried oregano, salt finely ground black pepper, and finely ground thyme from each side.
2. Leave the bacon for 2-3 minutes to make it soak the spices.
3. Then, Heat the air fryer to 360ºF.
4. Place the cut bacon in the air fryer rack and cook it for 5 minutes.
5. Then, turn the cut bacon to another side and cook it for 5 minutes more.
6. Then shred Cheddar cheese.
7. When the bacon is prepared – coat it with the minced cheese and cook for 30 seconds more.
8. Then move the cooked bacon to the plates.
9. Enjoy the breakfast immediately!

Nutrition:

Calories 423, Fat 33.1, Fiber 0.2, Carbs 1.5, Protein 28.1

## 24. MINI MOZZARELLA CHEESE BALLS

Preparation Time: 12 minutes
Cooking Time: 3 minutes
Servings: 5
Ingredients for 1 person:

- 8 oz. mozzarella balls
- 1 egg
- ½ cup coconut flakes
- ½ cup almond flour
- 1 teaspoon thyme
- 1 teaspoon finely ground black pepper
- 1 teaspoon paprika to taste

Directions:

1. Beat the egg in the small bowl and whisk it.
2. Then, mix the coconut flour with the thyme, finely ground black pepper, and paprika to taste. Slowly stir it carefully.
3. Then coat Mozzarella balls with coconut flakes.
4. Then, move the balls to the whisked egg mixture and coat them in the almond flour mixture.
5. Place Mozzarella balls in the freezer for 5 minutes.
6. Then, Heat the air fryer to 400ºF.
7. Place the frozen cheese balls in the heated air fryer and cook them for 3 minutes.
8. After the due time – remove the cheese tots from the air fryer basket and chill them for 2 minutes.
9. Serve the dish!

Nutrition:

Calories 166, Fat 12.8, Fiber 1.4, Carbs 2.8, Protein 9.5

## GUIDED MEDITATION 3

Focus on the attention while sitting in Vajrasana with heels pointing outward and big toes touching. Place the palms on the floor beside the buttocks and fingers pointing to the front. Next, slowly bend back and bring down your head to the ground while arching the back. Place your hands on your thighs and try to keep the lower legs connected with the ground. Proceed to close your eyes and relax your body, breathing deeply and slowly. Release by shifting your weight onto the left arm and elbow while slowly returning to the Vajrasana position. One important note is that it is not good to leave the ultimate position by straightening the legs first as it can dislocate the knee joints. Continue to repeat the process three to five times, and you can increase the process eight to 10 times after you have mastered the process.

## 25. OATMEAL VANILLA SHAKE

Preparation Time: 5 minutes
Cooking Time: 0 minutes
Servings: 1

Ingredients for 1 person:
- ¼ teaspoon vanilla extract
- 1 tablespoon oatmeal
- ½ teaspoon ground cinnamon
- 1 cup low-fat nut milk
- 1 scoop of vanilla whey protein powder

Directions:
1. Add the vanilla, oatmeal, cinnamon, milk, and protein powder to a blender. Mix everything. If you want your shake to be thicker, you can add some ice.
2. Pour the shake into a glass. If you want, you can serve it with a dusting of cinnamon, a couple of nuts, or a squirt of low-fat cream.

Nutrition:
Calories: 179, Fat: 5.1 g, Protein: 23.5 g, Carb: 8.3 g

## 26. SCRAMBLED EGGS WITH BLACK BEAN PUREE

Preparation Time: 5 minutes
Cooking Time: 10 minutes
Servings: 1

Ingredients for 1 person:
- 1 tablespoon unflavored whey protein powder
- 2 tablespoons vegetable or chicken broth
- 3 tablespoons green enchilada sauce
- ½ cup rinsed black beans
- Egg
- Pepper
- Salt

Directions:
1. After you have rinsed off your black beans, add them to a small pot and let them heat over medium.
2. Add in two and a half tablespoons of the enchilada sauce to your beans and stir them. Allow the mixture to cook for another two minutes.
3. Mix in the chicken broth.
4. Add the black bean mixture to your blender and mix it until completely smooth.
5. Make sure you are careful because the mixture is hot.
6. If you have an immersion blender, you can use that as well to puree the beans.
7. Pour the pureed beans into a bowl.
8. Allow the pureed beans to cool slightly, and then mix in the protein powder until well combined.
9. Cover them to keep them warm until you have cooked your egg.
10. Refrigerate whatever you have left.
11. Heat a pan on medium-high, and as it is warming, whisk the egg together with the pepper and salt until it is well incorporated.
12. Pour the mixed egg into the hot pan. With a rubber spatula, slowly scramble the eggs until cooked all the way through.
13. Once the egg is nearly cooked but still has a liquid texture, fold it onto itself and then place it on a plate.
14. Top your egg with a tablespoon of the black bean puree you made earlier, and then pour the remaining green enchilada sauce on top.

Nutrition:
Calories: 308, Fat: 5.2 g, Protein: 42.9 g, Carb: 22.6 g

## 27. FROZEN MOCHA FRAPPUCCINO

Preparation Time: 5 minutes
Cooking Time: 0 minutes
Servings: 1

Ingredients for 1 person:
- Low-sugar chocolate syrup (optional)
- Low-fat whipped cream (optional)
- 1 cup ice
- 1 tablespoon cocoa powder
- 3-4 drops liquid sweetener
- ½ cup 0% fat Greek yogurt
- ¼ cup unsweetened almond milk
- ¼ cup brewed coffee

Directions:
1. Add the ice, cocoa, sweetener, yogurt, milk, and coffee to your blender and pulse it a few times to mix everything extremely well.
2. Pour your Frappuccino into a tall glass and top it with some whipped cream and chocolate syrup if desired. Enjoy.

Nutrition:
Calories: 93, Fat: 2.7 g, Protein: 11.8 g, Carb: 4.84 g

## 28. BLACK BEAN AND LIME PUREE

Preparation Time: 5 minutes
Cooking Time: 10 minutes
Servings: 1

Ingredients for 1 person:
- 1 tablespoon unflavored protein powder
- ¼ cup vegetable or chicken broth
- ½ tablespoon jarred jalapeno juice
- ½ tablespoon lime juice
- ¼ cup rinsed black beans

Directions:
1. After you have rinsed your black beans, place them into a small pot and allow them to heat over medium.
2. Mix in the juice from the jalapenos and the lime juice. Stir everything together and allow it to heat through.
3. Once heated, mix in the chicken broth.
4. Pour the mixture into the blender and mix until it is completely smooth. Be careful because the mixture is hot, and make sure that you hold the lid.
5. If you have an immersion blender, you can use that as well. Pour the mixture into a bowl.
6. Allow the mixture to cool slightly and then mix in the protein powder until it is well mixed.
7. Enjoy.

Nutrition:
Calories: 180, Fat: 1.9 g, Protein: 30.6 g, Carb: 11.6 g

## 29. CHOCOLATE PB2 BANANA PROTEIN SHAKE
by Shannon Harms – Albuquerque

Preparation Time: 10 minutes
Cooking Time: 0 minutes
Servings: 2

Ingredients for 1 person:
- 4-5 ice cubes
- 1 Frozen sliced banana
- ¼ cup chocolate whey isolate protein powder
- ¼ cup PB2 powder
- 1 cup light soy milk

Directions:
1. Place all of the ingredients in a high-speed blender and mix until everything is smooth and creamy.

Nutrition:
Calories: 319, Fat: 4.9 g, Protein: 40.8 g, Carb: 32.6 g

## 30. PUMPKIN PROTEIN SMOOTHIE
by Maria Smith – Morehead City

Preparation Time: 5 minutes
Cooking Time: 5 minutes
Servings: 2

Ingredients for 1 person:
- 1 cup ice cubes
- ¼ teaspoon pumpkin pie spice
- ¼ teaspoon cinnamon
- ¼ cup vanilla whey protein powder
- 1/3 cup pumpkin puree
- ¾ cup soy milk
- ½ cup vanilla Greek frozen yogurt
- Frozen banana

Directions:
1. Place all ingredients into your blender and mix on high for around two to three minutes, or until it is smooth. Scrape the sides down as needed.
2. Add a little extra milk if your mixture is too thick. If it's too thin, add extra ice cubes.

Nutrition:
Calories: 254, Fat: 3.7 g, Protein: 27.9 g, Carb: 28.7 g

## 31. APPLE CUCUMBER JUICE
by John Terhune – Enosburg Falls

Preparation Time: 5 minutes
Cooking Time: 0 minutes
Servings: 4

Ingredients for 1 person:
- 1 Head romaine lettuce
- 3 small mandarin oranges
- 1 Lime
- 1 Large lemon
- 1 Large cucumber
- 3 medium apples

Directions:
1. You will need a juicer for this recipe.
2. Wash all of the fruits and veggies very well. This is because you are going to be using the skins as well.

3. Run the fruits and veggies through your juice. This makes 32 ounces of juice.

**Nutrition:**
Calories: 146, Fat: .8 g, Protein: 2 g, Carb: 38.4 g

## 32. VITAMIN C JUICE
by Mary Burns – Tukwila

Preparation Time: 5 minutes
Cooking Time: 0 minutes
Servings: 4

**Ingredients for 1 person:**
- Handful ginger
- ¼ pineapple
- 2 limes
- 1 lemon
- 5 grapefruits

**Directions:**
1. Remove the tops and bottoms from the grapefruits. With a sharp knife, cut around the edges of the peeling. Make sure you don't cut away the pith. This holds a lot of nutrients.
2. Do the same thing with the lemon, limes, and pineapple. If you have a high-quality juicer, you don't have to worry about peeling the lemon and lime.
3. Juice the grapefruits, ginger, limes, and lemon. Lastly, juice the pineapple.
4. Serve over ice and enjoy.

**Nutrition:**
Calories: 88, Fat: .4 g, Protein: 1.7 g, Carb: 23.6 g

## 33. CHERRY MANGO SMOOTHIE
by Melanie D. Henn – Fort Walton Beach

Preparation Time: 10 minutes
Cooking Time: 5 minutes
Servings: 1

**Ingredients for 1 person:**
- ¾ cup water
- 1 cup frozen mango
- ½ cup water
- 1 cup frozen sweeten cherries

**Directions:**
1. Allow the mangoes and cherries to sit in separate bowls until they are thawed, which should take around ten minutes.
2. Add the cherries to a blender with half a cup of water and blend until smooth. Add in a little more water if it seems too thick. Pour the mixture into a glass.
3. Rinse out the blender and add the mango and remaining water. Blend until smooth, adding more water if you need to. Pour this over the cherries and enjoy.

**Nutrition:**
Calories: 185, Fat: 0 g, Protein: 2 g, Carb: 46 g

## 34. COCO-RITA COCKTAIL
by Melanie D. Henn – Fort Walton Beach

Preparation Time: 5 minutes
Cooking Time: 0 minutes
Servings: 1

**Ingredients for 1 person:**
- 2 tablespoons squeezed orange juice
- 4 tablespoons coconut water
- 2 tablespoons healthy sugar replacement
- 5 tablespoons lime juice
- Rock salt
- Lime wedges

**Directions:**
1. Get a martini glass and run a wedge of lime around the edge, then dip the glass in salt.
2. Add the orange juice, coconut water, syrup, and lime juice to a shaker and shake vigorously for about 20 seconds.
3. Add ice to your martini glass and strain the drink over the ice. Serve with a lime wedge and edible flower if desired.

**Nutrition:**
Calories: 24, Fat: 0.1 g, Protein: 0.4 g, Carb: 5.7

## GUIDED MEDITATION 4

Find a comfortable position, either laying down or sitting. Take in three deep and slow breaths. With each inhale, imagine the breath sending energy to the space right above your belly button. With every exhale, release whatever you are holding in this area. This could be pain or fear. It could even be what you think you should feel while in this meditation. You can place your hand on this area while you meditate if you like.

Begin to gently tap the area above your belly button with two fingers. You can also gently massage the area in a circular motion.

As you continue to breathe in and out through your nose, direct your breath to your chakra. Picture a yellow glowing light growing and pulsing in your upper abdomen area. For people who identify mostly as male, the light should spin clockwise. For people who identify mostly as female, the light should spin counterclockwise.

If you start to feel a new awareness in your solar plexus chakra, something like a pulsating in this area, you have made a connection to your solar plexus chakra.

As your meditation comes to a close, take three deep and slow breaths. Direct your

# PERSONAL NOTES

# PERSONAL NOTES

# CHAPTER 10
## BREAKFAST

BE PART OF THIS COMMUNITY OF CRAZY INNOVATORS AND SHARE YOUR
UNCONVENTIONAL KNOWLEDGE...BE PART OF ...
FUN CLUB KITCHEN

## 35. BERRY CHEESECAKE OVERNIGHT OATS

Preparation Time: 5 minutes
Cooking Time: 5 minutes
Servings: 1
Ingredients for 1 person:
- ½ cup fresh (or frozen, thawed) blueberries
- 1 teaspoon honey
- ½ teaspoon vanilla extract
- ½ cup rolled oats
- ½ cup low-fat cottage cheese
- ½ cup unsweetened almond milk
- 12 almonds, chopped

Directions:
1. In a bowl or container, mix berries, nectar, vanilla, and squash with a fork. Include oats, curds, and almond milk, and mix to combine. (The blend will be thick and might appear to be dry, yet the oats will soften as they sit.)
2. Refrigerate in any event 6hrs.
3. Serving cold sprinkled with almonds.

Nutrition:
Calories: 406, Carbs: 48 g, Sugar: 11 g, Protein: 24 g

## 36. PUMPKIN PROTEIN PANCAKES

Preparation Time: 10 minutes
Cooking Time: 10 minutes
Servings: 2
Ingredients for 1 person:
- 2 large eggs
- ¾ cup plain 2% fat Greek yogurt
- ½ cup canned pumpkin
- 1 ½ tablespoons maple syrup, divided
- ½ teaspoon vanilla extract
- ½ cup whole wheat flour
- ¼ cup rolled oats
- 1 teaspoon baking powder
- 1 pinch salt
- ¼ teaspoon pumpkin pie spice
- 20 pecan halves, chopped

Directions:
1. In a bowl, beat eggs. Blend in yogurt, pumpkin, 1 tablespoon maple syrup, and vanilla.
2. In another bowl, blend flour, oats, preparing powder, salt, and pumpkin pie flavor.
3. Add dry ingredients to wet and blend to consolidate.
4. In an enormous nonstick skillet covered with a cooking splash over medium-low heat, drop a loading 1/3 cup hitter for every flapjack. Cook until the underside is darker and air pockets structure on top, around 3 minutes. Flip and cook around 3 minutes more. Rehash with the residual hitter.
5. Top with walnut parts and the rest of the maple syrup.
6. Cool extra hotcakes before putting them away in an impenetrable holder in the ice chest for as long as 3 days or store the remaining hitter in a sealed shut compartment in the ice chest for as long as 4 days.

Nutrition:
Calories: 415, Carbs: 49 g, Sugar: 15 g, Protein: 22 g

## 37. AVOCADO TOAST WITH COTTAGE CHEESE & TOMATOES

Preparation Time: 5 minutes
Cooking Time: 5 minutes
Servings: 4
Ingredients for 1 person:
- 8 slices hearty whole grain bread
- 2 cups cottage cheese low fat
- 1 ripe California avocado sliced
- 1 tomato sliced
- Salt and freshly cracked pepper to taste

Directions:
1. Lay bread cuts out on an enormous cutting board and top each one with ¼ cup of curds. Sprinkle with salt and pepper.
2. Top curds with avocado and tomato cut at that point season with another spot of salt and pepper.
3. Cut bread cuts down the middle and serve.

Nutrition:
Calories: 440, Fat: 11.9 g, Carb: 63.5 g, Protein: 25 g

## 38. SAVORY PARMESAN OATMEAL

Preparation Time: 10 minutes
Cooking Time: 35 minutes
Servings: 1
Ingredients for 1 person:
- 1 cup unsweetened almond milk
- 2/3 cup rolled oats
- ½ cup kale leaves, chopped

- ½ cup broccoli florets, chopped
- Salt
- Pepper
- 1 oz. Parmesan cheese, grated

Directions:

1  In a touch pot, warm temperature almond milk, 1/3 cup water, oats, kale, and broccoli. Season with salt and pepper.

2  Heat to the point of boiling, at that thing, decrease to stew and prepare dinner, blending at instances, till oats are whole, kale is withered, and broccoli is cooked although the pretty company, 5 to 7 minutes.

3  Top with parmesan.

Nutrition:

Calories: 392, Carbs: 45 g, Sugar: 3 g, Protein: 21 g

## 39. STRAWBERRY CHEESECAKE CHIA SEED PUDDING

Preparation Time: 10 minutes
Cooking Time: 0 minutes
Servings: 1
Ingredients for 1 person:

- ¼ cup Cottage cheese
- 1 tablespoon Greek yogurt
- 1 cup chopped strawberries, divided
- ½ cup almond milk
- 1/8 teaspoon vanilla
- 2 teaspoons raw sugar
- 2 teaspoons chia seeds

Directions:

1  In a blender, join the curds, Greek yogurt, 1/2 cup strawberries, almond milk, vanilla, and crude sugar, and mix until the blend is totally smooth and lovably pink. You may need to scratch down with a spatula once in the middle.

2  Fill a lidded holder and include the chia seeds, mixing admirably. Let sit medium-term (at any rate 24 hours, the more it sets, the thicker it gets!) In the cooler.

3  The following day when you are prepared to eat it, blend it again to appropriate the seeds equitably and present with the staying 1/2 cup slashed strawberries. Yum

Nutrition:

Calories: 24, Total fat: 8 g

## 40. MOCHA BANANA PROTEIN SMOOTHIE BOWL

Preparation Time: 5 minutes
Cooking Time: 0 minutes
Servings: 1
Ingredients for 1 person:

- 1 large frozen banana
- ½ cup almond breeze chocolate almond milk, plus more if necessary
- 1 scoop your favorite protein powder
- 1 packet instant coffee, if desired
- 1 cup spinach
- A few cubes of ice

Toppings:

- Almond butter
- Toasted almonds
- Chia seeds
- Low-fat granola
- Sliced bananas
- Fresh strawberries
- Carob chips
- Unsweetened coconut flakes

Directions:

1  Include all fixings aside from wanted garnishes to a blender and mix until smooth and rich. On the off chance that is fundamental, include more almond milk and additionally ice to arrive at the ideal consistency. The smoothie ought to be genuinely thick so you can eat it with a spoon.

2  Fill a bowl and top with wanted garnishes, for example, chia and granola.

Nutrition:

Calories: 272, Fat: 4 g, Carb: 45 g, Sugar: 26.6 g, Protein: 20 g

## 41. APPLE PIE OATMEAL

Preparation Time: 5 minutes
Cooking Time: 25 minutes
Servings: 1
Ingredients for 1 person:

- 1 cup 2% milk
- ½ medium apple, cored and chopped
- 1/3 cup rolled oats
- 1 teaspoon maple syrup

- ¼ teaspoon vanilla extract
- 1 pinch cinnamon
- 1 pinch salt
- 20 almonds, chopped

Directions:

1. In a bit pot, be part of milk and cleaved apple. Heat to the point of boiling, lessen to a stew and prepare dinner, mixing sometimes, until apple starts evolved to relax, round 5 minutes.
2. Include oats, syrup, vanilla, cinnamon, and salt. Heat to the factor of boiling, at that factor, lessen to a stew and cook until oats are full, 5 to 7 minutes extra.
3. Top with slashed almonds.

Nutrition:

Calories: 413, Fat: 18 g, Carbs: 49 g, Sugar: 25 g, Protein: 17 g

## 42. PUMPKIN APPLE FRENCH TOAST BAKE

Preparation Time: 10 minutes
Cooking Time: 40 minutes
Servings: 3
Ingredients for 1 person:

- 6 large eggs
- ½ cup canned pumpkin
- tablespoons almond butter
- 1 tablespoon maple syrup
- 1 teaspoon vanilla extract
- ½ teaspoon cinnamon
- slices whole-wheat bread, cut into 1-inch pieces
- 1 medium apple, cored and very thinly sliced

Directions:

1. Warm broiler to 375°F.
2. In a bowl, whisk eggs, pumpkin, almond butter, maple syrup, vanilla, and cinnamon. Include bread until the egg mixture is absorbed. Blend in apple.
3. Coat a little broiler-safe skillet (ideally cast iron) or 8-inch round cake container with a cooking spray. Cautiously pour bread mixture into skillet, and press into an even layer.
4. Prepare until cooked through, puffed, and marginally caramelized on top, 30 to 35 minutes. Cool somewhat before serving.
5. Cool remains totally before putting away in a water/airproof holder in the refrigerator.

Nutrition:

Calories: 411, Carbs: 43 g, Sugar: 16 g, Protein: 21 g

## 43. BLUEBERRY GREEK YOGURT PANCAKES

Preparation Time: 15 minutes
Cooking Time: 25 minutes
Servings: 2
Ingredients for 1 person:

- 2 large eggs
- ¾ cup plain 2% fat Greek yogurt
- 1 ½ tablespoon honey, divided
- ½ teaspoon vanilla extract
- ½ cup whole wheat flour
- 1 teaspoon baking powder
- 1 pinch salt
- ¼ teaspoon cinnamon
- 1 cup fresh (or frozen, thawed) blueberries
- 2 tablespoons natural peanut butter, divided

Directions:

1. In a bowl, beat eggs. Blend in yogurt, 1/2 tablespoon nectar, and vanilla. In another bowl, mix flour, heating powder, salt, and cinnamon. Add dry ingredients to wet and blend to combine. Blend in 1/2 cup blueberries.
2. In a big nonstick skillet covered with a cooking spray over medium-low heat, drop a stacking 1/4 cup hitter for every flapjack. Cook until the underside is dark-colored and air pockets structure on top, around 3 minutes. Flip and cook for around 3 minutes more. Rehash with the residual player.
3. Top each presentation with 1/2 tablespoon nectar, 1 tablespoon nutty spread, and 1/4 cup blueberries.

Nutrition:

Calories: 436, Carbs: 54 g, Sugar: 25 g, Protein: 23 g

## 44. BLACKBERRY ALMOND BUTTER SANDWICH

Preparation Time: 30 minutes
Cooking Time: 0 minutes
Servings: 1
Ingredients for 1 person:

- ¼ cup blackberries
- 1 teaspoon chia seeds
- 2 slices 100% whole wheat bread, lightly toasted
- 2 tablespoons natural almond butter

Directions:

1   In a bowl, pound blackberries softly with a fork. Mix in chia seeds.

2   Discretionary: cover and refrigerate blackberry-chia blend for as long as 4 days for a thick, jam-like consistency.

3   Collect sandwich with blackberry blend more than one cut of bread and almond margarine over another cut.

**Nutrition:**

Calories: 445, Fat: 19 g, Carbs: 52 g, Sugar 11 g, Protein: 19 g

## 45. BLACKBERRY VANILLA FRENCH TOAST

**Preparation Time:** 10 minutes
**Cooking Time:** 50 minutes
**Servings:** 2
**Ingredients for 1 person:**

- 4 eggs, beaten
- ½ teaspoon vanilla extract
- Salt
- 4 slices whole-wheat bread
- 1 cup fresh blackberries
- 20 pecan halves, chopped
- 2 teaspoons maple syrup

**Directions:**

1   In a shallow dish, mix eggs, vanilla, and a gap of salt altogether. Absorb cuts of bread egg blend, every cut in flip, till all of the egg is retained.

2   In a big nonstick skillet protected with cooking, bathe over medium warm temperature, consist of the two drenched bread cuts, and cook dinner until underside is awesome darker around 3 minutes. Flip and prepare dinner until fantastic dark-colored and quite firm, around 3 minutes extra.

3   Rehash with the staying bread cuts and the rest of the egg combination.

4   Top with blackberries, walnuts, and maple syrup.

**Nutrition:**

Calories 434, Fat 17 g, Carbs 49 g, Sugar 14 g, Protein 22 g

## 46. CHOCOLATE-PEANUT BUTTER FRENCH TOAST

**Preparation Time:** 25 minutes
**Cooking Time:** 0 minutes
**Servings:** 1
**Ingredients for 1 person:**

- 1/3 cup liquid egg whites
- 2 teaspoons unsweetened cocoa powder
- ½ teaspoon vanilla extract
- Salt
- 2 slices whole-grain bread
- 1 tablespoon peanut butter
- 2/3 cup fresh raspberries

**Directions:**

1   In a shallow dish or bowl, whisk collectively egg whites, cocoa powder, vanilla, and a touch of salt. Absorb bread egg blend, each reduced in flip, until all the egg is absorbed.

2   In a giant, nonstick skillet blanketed with cooking splash over medium warmth, consist of bread cuts and cook dinner until underside is dim brilliant darker, around 3 minutes. Flip and cook until terrific darkish colored and marginally firm, round 3 minutes greater.

3   Spread nutty unfold on French toast. Top with raspberries.

**Nutrition:**

Calories 404, Carbs 52 g, Protein 21 g

## GUIDED MEDITATION 5

Begin with a light stretch to relax the muscles for your meditation.

Stand up and lift your hands into the air as if you are reaching up to touch the sky.

Reach as far as you can while you take a deep breath in, holding the position and your breath for two seconds.

As you exhale, drop your hands to your sides, for another two seconds.

Lift your hands again as you breathe in and drop them to your sides as you exhale.

Repeat at least three times before proceeding with the meditation.

Sit up in a comfortable position on the floor or a chair in the room of your sacral chakra meditation healing practice.

Cross your legs, as you extend your spine nice and straight.

Lift your head, as if you are balancing a book right on top.

Place your hands on your knees with the palms facing upwards.

Get rid of any distractions, by closing the windows, turning off your phone, and locking the doors.

Start your meditation by breathing slowly and deeply while staring off into space.

Take as long as you need to relax your body and muscles, adjust your mind from wandering around, and gently allow your eyes to slowly close.

Further, bring your body to relaxation by focusing on and relaxing different parts of your body such as legs, stomach, chest, arms, shoulders, neck, and head, as you move your focus along your body from top to bottom.

Take a couple of seconds to hold the image of yourself sitting up while relaxing your body.

You can also direct your focus to how your chest and body rise taller as you breathe in or fall shorter as you breathe out.

Hold your attention on your breathing to ensure that your mind won't slip away.

By bringing your focus somewhere else except your mind, you can clear your thoughts from any worries or troubles.

Now that your body is close to its relaxed state and so is your mind change the way you breathe to fit the opening of the solar plexus area.

Since the location of the chakra is on the lower part of your ribs, you will be using your chest to breathe.

Inhale the air and expand your lungs, hold your breath for at least four seconds before exhaling through your mouth.

Visualize releasing any negativity through your exhale as your spine expands higher every time you breathe.

Focus on the way your chest rises and falls and don't let your mind wander away.

If it does, then gently bring your attention back to the movement of your spine.

Visualize channeling your energy and centering it on the palm of your hands.

Place your hands on the area above your belly button but below your heart.

You will be touching the lower part of your ribs.

You should place your hands next to each other and not overlap each other.

Concentrate on making the energy flow through your hands and to the solar plexus.

Visualize it healing the chakra, clearing it of any blockage, and releasing the negative emotions or negative tensions that could affect the physical health of the body, imagine anything negative leaving through your mouth as you exhale.

When you are sitting down, start to connect and feel the coldness or warmth of the floor, the bed, or the ground beneath you.

Visualize the energy from the ground traveling up through your body, through your toes.

Imagine sucking in that energy that belongs to the earth.

Focus on this energy as it's moving up towards the location of the solar plexus which is in between your belly button and the bottom of your rib cage, also known as the upper abdomen.

With your hands still on the upper abdomen, imagine a yellow glow forming and expanding in that area as all the energy begin connecting, rotating clockwise, and getting larger every time you take a breath in.

Feel the warmth and sensation that the yellow light is providing and how it makes you feel emotional.

Keep your hands on that area for at least two to three minutes before moving on and placing your hands on the top of your knees, forming a mudra by touching both the thumb and the index finger together.

If you'd like, you can keep cleansing the area for longer than three minutes, however long you feel is necessary for your upper abdomen to heal.

Begin to imagine that you are sitting on top of a grassy hill, sitting right below the sun that is shining right back down on you.

The energy tingles within your upper abdomen, experiencing healing and cleansing.

Focus your attention on the part of your body that you imagine is the warmest from the sun, such as the top of your head.

Yellow stimulates feelings of joy, and it also represents the solar plexus.

Feel and appreciate the warmth you are receiving and accept the tingling sensations spreading through your body.

Then start to bring your attention inwards, notice how the ground beneath you feels like, is it cold or warm?

Can you feel any tingling or pulses through it?

What about the space above your head?

Does it feel like a whole universe is right above you just by feeling a little pressure on your head?

Freely lift your arms towards the sky as you inhale and feel the astral world above you.

Picture a bright yellow flame at the tip of your fingers, feel as it connects through your hands and travels down to your upper abandonment where the solar plexus is located.

Breathe out and lower your arms down to the ground.

Place your hands on the ground and feel the earth beneath you and the perfect balance of life and energy around you.

Inhale once more, raising your hands towards the sky as if connecting your energy with the one with the sun.

Let the yellow glow travel down to your upper abandonment, clearing and opening that chakra point.

Notice what you are feeling during this moment, are you feel calm, balanced, and happy?

Repeat the hand motions for a few minutes or however long you wish.

Place your hands back down on your knees, forming the mudra. Use the mantra 'ram' by saying it out loud physically.

This specific mantra vibrates the body and helps the negative energies flow out of the chakra and out of the body while leaving only positive and pure healing forces.

Mantras are just words that are said during meditations, but they can also be used in practices to ensure that the body is cleared effectively.

Place one of your hands on your back, with the palm facing outwards while you repeat the same process of visualizing the yellow energy healing, moving, and releasing any tensions in the upper abdomen.

Take a minute to rest in the healing sensations.

To finish, place your hands back on the ground.

Breathe in deeply with an open mind for a minute while bringing your awareness back to the physical world.

Imagine the room that you are in to help get back to your consciousness and the body.

Make an intention to express utmost gratitude to the Universe for guiding your energy, for healing you, and opening your solar plexus chakra.

Take another minute to simply breathe in deeply, in through your nose, and out through your mouth.

Open your eyes slowly but do not move your body.

Look around you, take in the details of your room, stay in the moment for a few minutes while reflecting on the healing that you just achieved.

## 47. WATERMELON QUINOA PARFAIT

Preparation Time: 15 minutes
Cooking Time: 20 minutes
Servings: 1

Ingredients for 1 person:
- 1 cup watermelon, cut into bite-sized pieces
- ½ cup cooked quinoa
- 1 tablespoon fresh mint, chopped
- ½ cup plain 2% fat Greek yogurt
- 20 almonds, chopped

Directions:
1. In a bowl, mix watermelon, quinoa, and mint.
2. In a container or bowl, layer watermelon-quinoa blend with yogurt.
3. Top with almonds.

Nutrition:
Calories 411, Fat 17 g, Carbs 42 g, Sugar 17 g, Protein 25 g

## 48. APPLE AND GOAT CHEESE SANDWICH

Preparation Time: 5 minutes
Cooking Time: 5 minutes
Servings: 1

Ingredients for 1 person:
- 2 slices 100% whole-wheat bread, toasted
- 1 oz. goat cheese, at room temperature
- 1 tablespoon natural peanut butter
- ½ medium apple, cored and thinly sliced, divided
- ¼ teaspoon cinnamon

Directions:
1 Spread 1 bit of toast with goat cheddar and the other with a nutty spread. Make a sandwich with a large portion of the apple cuts sprinkled with cinnamon.
2 Present with residual apple cuts.

Nutrition:
Calories 408, Fat 17 g, Carb 49 g, Sugar 15 g, Protein 17 g

## 49. CARROT CAKE OATMEAL

Preparation Time: 5 minutes
Cooking Time: 50 minutes
Servings: 1

Ingredients for 1 person:
- ½ cup unsweetened almond milk
- 1 small carrot, peeled and finely grated
- 1/3 cup rolled oats
- 1 tablespoon raisins
- 1 teaspoon honey
- ¼ teaspoon vanilla extract
- 1 pinch cinnamon
- 1 pinch salt
- 1 ½ tablespoon peanut butter
- 1/3 cup low-fat Cottage cheese

Directions:
1 1 In a bit pot, mix almond milk, half cup of water, carrot, oats, raisins, nectar, vanilla, cinnamon, and salt. Heat to the factor of boiling, at that point, reduce to stew and cook, mixing occasionally, until thick and oats are stout, 5 to 7 minutes.
2 Blend inside the nutty unfold and take out from the heat.
3 Top cereal with curds and extra cinnamon.

Nutrition:

Calories 423, Fat 17 g, Carbs 51 g, Protein 21 g

## 50. COCONUT CRANBERRY PROTEIN BARS

**Preparation Time:** 20 minutes
**Cooking Time:** 0 minutes
**Servings:** 1
**Ingredients for 1 person:**
- ¼ cup unsweetened shredded coconut flakes
- ¼ cup organic dried cranberries
- ¼ cup almond butter
- 2 tablespoons almond meal
- 2 tablespoons flax meal
- 3 tablespoons coconut oil
- 1 tablespoon raw honey
- 2 eggs
- 6 scoops of coconut fuel protein
- Dash Himalayan sea salt
- Optional: 1/4 organic dark chocolate chunks/enjoy life's chocolate chips

Directions:
1. Preheat stove to 350ºF
2. Come to all fixings in a bowl and blend until a batter-like consistency
3. Line an 8x8 preparing dish with material paper
4. Take off batter into a level and even square
5. Prepare for 15 to 20 minutes or until somewhat solidified
6. Let cool and cut into squares

**Nutrition:**
Calories 214, Fat 12.2 g, Carb 8.2 g, Sugars 3.1 g, Protein 20 g

## 51. EGG WHITE OATMEAL WITH STRAWBERRIES AND PEANUT BUTTER

**Preparation Time:** 5 minutes
**Cooking Time:** 10 minutes
**Servings:** 1
**Ingredients for 1 person:**
- ½ cup rolled oats
- ½ cup unsweetened almond milk
- 6 large fresh (or frozen, thawed) strawberries, cored and chopped
- 2 teaspoons honey
- ½ teaspoon vanilla extract
- 1 pinch salt
- 1/3 cup liquid egg whites
- 1 tablespoon peanut butter

**Directions:**
1. In a little pot, heat oats, 1/2 cup almond milk, 1/3 cup water, strawberries, nectar, vanilla, and salt. Heat to the point of boiling, at that point, decrease to stew and cook, blending once in a while, until the blend is thick and oats are full, 5 to 7 minutes. Expel from warm.
2. In a bowl, whisk egg whites until somewhat bubbly. Add cooked cereal to egg whites a spoonful at once, rushing between every option until oats are completely joined.
3. Pour blend once more into the pot and cook over low heat, always mixing, until oats are thick, 2 to 3 minutes. Be mindful so as not to turn the warmth excessively high, so eggs don't scramble.
4. Top cereal with nutty spread.

**Nutrition:**
Calories 412, Carbs 51 g, Sugar 17 g, Protein 20 g

## 52. AVOCADO SHRIMP SALAD

**Preparation Time:** 15 Minutes
**Cooking Time:** 0 minutes
**Servings:** 4
**Ingredients for 1 person:**
- 1 ripe avocado
- 1 tablespoon Tabasco
- 1 teaspoon ranch dressing
- ½ cup yogurt
- 1 lb. shrimp, cooked
- 1 grapefruit, cut into sections

**Directions:**
1. Combine Tabasco, ranch dressing, and yogurt.
2. Place shrimp, avocado, and grapefruit in a large bowl.
3. Pour dressing over shrimp and avocado mixture.
4. Serve and enjoy.

**Nutrition:**
Calories: 226, Fat: 10.2 g, Carbohydrates: 11.2 g, Sugar: 4.7 g, Protein: 24.2 g, Cholesterol: 164 mg

## 53. EASY BAKED SALMON

**Preparation Time:** 9 minutes

**Cooking Time:** 16 minutes
**Servings:** 4
**Ingredients for 1 person:**
- 4 salmon fillets
- 1 lemon zest
- 1 teaspoon sea salt
- 3 oz. olive oil
- 1 garlic clove, minced
- 1 teaspoon fresh dill, chopped
- 1 tablespoon fresh parsley, chopped
- 1/8 teaspoon white pepper

**Directions:**
1. Preheat the oven at 200°C.
2. Place all ingredients except salmon fillet in a microwave-safe bowl and microwave for 45 seconds.
3. Stir well until combined.
4. Place salmon fillets on a parchment-lined baking dish.
5. Spread evenly olive oil and herb mixture over each salmon fillet.
6. Place in preheated oven and bake for 15 minutes.
7. Serve and enjoy.

**Nutrition:**
Calories: 408, Fat: 30.9 g, Carbohydrates: 0.5 g, Sugar: 0 g, Protein: 34.7 g, Cholesterol: 78 mg

## 54. MUSHROOM STRATA AND TURKEY SAUSAGE
by Patricia Ensley – Washington

**Preparation Time:** 15 minutes
**Cooking Time:** 60 minutes
**Servings:** 12
**Ingredients for 1 person:**
- 8 oz. cubed ciabatta bread
- 12 oz. chopped turkey sausage
- 2 cups milk
- 4 oz. shredded Cheddar
- 3 eggs
- 12 oz. egg substitute
- ½ cup chopped green onion
- 1 cup sliced mushroom
- ½ teaspoon paprika
- ½ teaspoon pepper
- 2 tablespoons grated parmesan cheese

**Directions:**
1. Set oven to 400°F. Lay bread cubes flat on a baking tray and set it to toast for about 8 min.
2. Meanwhile, add a skillet over medium heat with sausage and allow to cook while stirring until fully brown and crumbled.
3. In a bowl, add pepper, parmesan cheese, egg substitute, salt, paprika, eggs, Cheddar cheese, and milk, then whisk to combine.
4. Add in remaining ingredients and toss well to incorporate. Transfer mixture to a large baking dish (preferably a 9x13-inch), then tightly cover and allow to rest in the refrigerator overnight.
5. Set oven to 350°F, remove the cover from the casserole dish and set to bake until fully cooked and golden brown.
6. Slice and serve.

**Nutrition:**
Calories: 185, Fat: 18 g, Carbohydrates: 9.2 g, Protein: 2.4 g

## 55. MILLET CONGEE
by Mary A. Worsley – Philadelphia

**Preparation Time:** 15 minutes
**Cooking Time:** 60 minutes
**Servings:** 4
**Ingredients for 1 person:**
- 1 cup millet
- 5 cups water
- 1 cup diced sweet potato
- 1 teaspoon cinnamon
- 2 tablespoons stevia
- 1 diced apple
- ¼ cup honey

**Directions:**
1. In a deep pot, add stevia, sweet potato, cinnamon, water, and millet, then stir to combine.
2. Bring to boil over high heat, then reduce to a simmer on low for an hour or until water is fully absorbed and millet is cooked.
3. Stir in remaining ingredients and serve.

**Nutrition:**
Calories: 136, Fat: 1 g, Carbs: 28.5 g, Protein: 3.1 g

## 56. AVOCADO CHERRY SMOOTHIE
by Jason Parente – Grand Rapids

Preparation Time: 5 minutes
Cooking Time: -
Servings: 3

**Ingredients for 1 person:**
- ½ ripe avocado, chopped
- 1 cup fresh cherries
- 1 cup coconut water, sugar-free
- 1 whole lime

**Directions:**
1. Peel the avocado and cut it in half. Remove the pit and chop it into bite-sized pieces. Reserve the rest in the refrigerator. Set aside.
2. Rinse the cherries under cold running water using a large colander. Cut each in half and remove the pits. Set aside.
3. Peel the lime and cut it in half. Set aside.
4. Now, combine avocado, cherries, coconut water, and lime in a blender. Pulse to combine and transfer to a serving glass.
5. Add a few ice cubes and refrigerate for 10 minutes before serving.

**Nutrition:**
Calories: 128, Protein: 1.7 g, Total Carbs: 17 g, Dietary Fibers: 3.8 g, Total Fat: 6.8 g

## 57. QUINOA BOWLS
by Annette J. York – Grand Rapids

Preparation Time: 10 minutes
Cooking Time: 25 minutes
Servings: 2

**Ingredients for 1 person:**
- 1 sliced peach
- 1/3 cup quinoa
- 1 cup low-fat milk
- ½ teaspoon vanilla extract
- 2 teaspoons natural stevia
- 12 raspberries
- 14 blueberries
- 2 teaspoons honey

**Directions:**
1. Add natural stevia, 2/3 cup milk, and quinoa to a saucepan, and stir to combine.
2. Over medium-high heat, bring to a boil, then cover and reduce heat to a low simmer for a further 20 minutes.
3. Grease and preheat grill to medium. Grill peach slices for about a minute per side. Set aside.
4. Heat remaining milk in the microwave and set aside.
5. Split cooked quinoa evenly between 2 serving bowls and top evenly with remaining ingredients. Enjoy!

**Nutrition:**
Calories: 180, Fat: 4 g, Carbs: 36 g, Protein: 4.5 g

## 58. BERRY MUESLI
by Patricia R Johns – Boston

Preparation Time: 6 hours 10 minutes
Cooking Time: 0 minutes
Servings: 2

**Ingredients for 1 person:**
- 1 cup oats
- 1 cup fruit-flavored yogurt
- ½ cup milk
- 1/8 teaspoon salt
- ½ cup dried raisins
- ½ cup chopped apple
- ½ cup frozen blueberries
- ¼ cup chopped walnuts

**Directions:**
1. Combine yogurt, salt, and oats in a medium bowl, mix well, and then cover the mixture tightly.
2. Place in the refrigerator to cool for 6 hours.
3. Add raisins and apples the gently fold.
4. Top with walnuts and serve.
5. Enjoy!

**Nutrition:**
Calories: 198, Carbs: 31.2 g, Fat: 4.3 g, Protein: 6 g

## 59. VANILLA EGG CUSTARD
by Shirley Gilliard – Boardman

Preparation Time: 10 Minutes
Cooking Time: 30 Minutes
Servings: 6

**Ingredients for 1 person:**
- 4 large eggs

- 2 teaspoons vanilla extract
- 2/3 cup Splenda
- 12 oz. can evaporated milk
- 1 cup milk
- ½ cup Nutmeg, grated

**Directions:**

1. Preheat the oven to 325°F.
2. Place six ramekins in a baking tray and set them aside.
3. Add vanilla, Splenda, eggs, evaporated milk, and milk in a blender and blend until smooth.
4. Pour mixture into the ramekins, then pour enough water into the baking tray and bake in a preheated oven for 30 minutes.
5. Serve chilled and enjoy.

**Nutrition:** Calories: 255, Fat: 8.4 g, Carbohydrates: 29.5 g, Sugar: 29.5 g, Protein: 9.4 g, Cholesterol: 144 mg

## 60. ASPARAGUS OMELET
by Crystal Hall – Denver

Preparation Time: 7 minutes
Cooking Time: 3 minutes
Servings: 2

**Ingredients for 1 person:**
- 4 asparagus spears, peel lower half
- 4 tablespoons parmesan cheese, grated
- 3 large eggs
- 2 teaspoons olive oil
- 1 garlic clove, minced
- Pepper
- Salt

**Directions:**

1. Heat olive oil in a pan over medium heat.
2. Add asparagus and garlic to the pan and sauté for 3 minutes.
3. Whisk eggs, cheese, 1 tablespoon water, pepper, and salt.
4. Pour egg mixture over the asparagus and cook until the desired doneness.
5. Serve and enjoy.

**Nutrition:** Calories: 159, Fat: 12.2 g, Carbohydrates: 3.0 g, Sugar: 1.5 g, Protein: 10.6 g, Cholesterol: 279 mg

## 61. STRAWBERRY & MUSHROOM SANDWICH
by Wanda Dobson – Phoenicia

Preparation Time: 10 minutes
Cooking Time: 0 minutes
Servings: 4

**Ingredients for 1 person:**
- 8 oz. cream cheese
- 1 tablespoon honey
- 1 tablespoon grated lemon zest
- 4 sliced Portobello mushrooms
- 2 cups sliced strawberries

**Directions:**

1. Add honey, lemon zest, and cheese to a food processor and process until fully incorporated.
2. Use cheese mixture to spread on mushrooms as you would butter.
3. Top with strawberries.
4. Enjoy!

**Nutrition:** Calories: 180, Fat: 16 g, Carbs: 6 g, Protein: 2 g

## GUIDED MEDITATION 6

Find a quiet, safe, and secluded space.

Begin by sitting in a cross-legged pose with your back and spine straight and your shoulders relaxed but held firmly back.

Raise both arms with the elbows bent at right angles.

On each hand, touch the fingers to the thumbs.

From the waist, rotate the upper body to the left while breathing in.

As you breathe out, rotate the upper body to the right

Repeat this exercise for as long as one minute.

# PERSONAL NOTES

# PERSONAL NOTES

# CHAPTER 11
# SOUPS AND SALADS

BE PART OF THIS COMMUNITY OF CRAZY INNOVATORS AND SHARE YOUR UNCONVENTIONAL KNOWLEDGE...BE PART OF ...
FUN CLUB KITCHEN

## 62. HAM & BEAN

Preparation Time: 10 min
Cooking Time: 4 hours
Servings: 10

Ingredients for 1 person:
- 125 ml celery, chopped fine
- 125 ml carrots, chopped fine
- 125 ml onion minced
- 1 garlic clove, minced
- 350 ml ham, cubed
- 1/8 teaspoon pepper, cayenne
- 1/4 teaspoon cumin, dried
- 1/4 teaspoon sea salt
- 1 can beans, navy
- 250 ml broth, chicken, or veggie
- 250 ml water

Directions:
1. Brown ham in a soup pot or large saucepan on medium heat.
2. Pour in water, scraping the glaze off the bottom of the pan.
3. Pour in the broth.
4. Add in the beans. Be sure to drain the liquid from the can and rinse the beans before adding.
5. Add in the remaining ingredients and stir well.
6. Bring soup to a boil, turn heat to simmer, and let it be for one to three hours (the longer it cooks, the better it tastes), stirring occasionally.

Nutrition:
Calories: 240, Carbohydrates: 25.8 g, Protein: 24.4 g, Fat: 4.1 g, Saturated Fat: 1.5 g, Polyunsaturated Fat: 3.6 g, Trans Fat: 0 g, Cholesterol: 30 mg, Sodium: 1044 mg, Fiber: 7 g, Sugar: 4.1 g

## 63. FRANK SINATRA SOUP

Preparation Time: 10 min
Cooking Time: 40 min
Servings: 10

Ingredients for 1 person:
- 1 tablespoon olive oil 1 onion, diced
- 4 cloves garlic, minced
- 250 ml carrots, diced
- 500 ml broccoli florets, chopped into small pieces
- 750 ml cauliflower florets, chopped into small pieces
- 1 - 1/2 liter of vegetable broth
- 4 tomatoes, medium, diced
- 1 tablespoon dried Italian herb mix
- Pinch red pepper flakes, crushed, a pinch
- Black pepper and salt for taste
- Parmesan cheese, grated, for sprinkling on top
- Fresh parsley, chopped, for sprinkling on top

Directions:
1. Heat the oil in a large soup pot over medium heat.
2. Add the garlic and onion. Cook until fragrant for about two min.
3. Stir in the carrot. Continue cooking time for another two-three min.
4. Pour in the broth, stir in the tomatoes, herbs, pinch of red pepper flakes, black pepper, and salt.
5. Bring the ingredients to a boil. Lower the heat and simmer for five min.
6. Add in the broccoli and cauliflower, simmering all the while until the vegetables are cooked through but still crunchy. This may take five min.
7. Taste and adjust your seasoning.
8. Serving yourself a bowl, sprinkling the cheese and parsley on top.

If you would like to enjoy this as a slightly thicker soup, stir one tablespoon of coconut flour or cornstarch into 75 ml of cold water. Add this to the soup and continue to cook for an additional 5 minutes after the vegetables have finished cooking time.

Nutrition:
Calories: 329, Carbohydrates: 43.6 g, Protein: 28.9 g, Fat: 4.9 g, Saturated Fat: 0.9 g, Polyunsaturated Fat: 4 g, Trans Fat: 0 g, Cholesterol: 64 mg, Sodium: 992 mg, Fiber: 9.3 g, Sugar: 5.8 g

## 64. ORANGE FIDELITY

Preparation Time: 20 min
Cooking Time: 45 min
Servings: 12

Ingredients for 1 person:
- 1 onion, medium, and sliced
- 2 pears, small, halved, unpeeled, cored, and chopped small
- 3 sprigs thyme
- 2 tablespoons olive oil, extra virgin

- 1 kilo butternut squash, halved, seeded, unpeeled
- 250 ml broth, chicken or vegetable
- 500 ml milk, non-fat

Garnish:
- 75 ml pecan pieces, toasted or almonds

Directions:
1. Heat oven to 400°F.
2. On a cookie sheet covered with parchment paper, place the pears, onions & thyme. Sprinkle with olive oil.
3. On top of this, place the two squash halves.
4. Roast for fifty-sixty min. It is done when you can pierce the squash with a fork. Remove from oven and let cool.
5. Scoop the flesh from the squash, discarding the peel.
6. Place squash flesh and pan contents (without the parchment paper) into a blender or food processor—blend.
7. Pour this into a large soup pot, add the broth, and simmer for ten min.
8. Stir in the milk and continue to simmer for another eight min.
9. Garnish with the nut pieces and servings.
10. Do not add the pecans as garnish unless you are more than six months post-directions.

Nutrition:
Calories: 144, Carbohydrates: 20.5 g, Protein: 0.5 g, Fat: 0.2 g, Saturated Fat: 0 g, Polyunsaturated Fat: 0 g, Trans Fat: 0 g, Cholesterol: 0 mg, Sodium: 41 mg, Fiber: 0.2 g, Sugar: 18 g

## 65. POTATO BROCCOLI SOUP

Preparation Time: 10 minutes
Cooking Time: 30 minutes
Servings: 8

Ingredients for 1 person:
- ½ cup broth
- Half a cup broccoli (chopped)
- 1 small-sized potato (chopped)
- 1 tablespoon corn starch
- ½ cup milk
- 2 tablespoons Cheddar cheese (shredded)
- 1 teaspoon garlic powder
- Pepper and salt to taste

Directions:
1. Peel and cut the potato. Then boil it until it becomes soft.
2. Steam the broccoli until it is tender.
3. Put the potato and broccoli in one food processor and make a puree.
4. Mix 1 tablespoon corn starch in 1/4th cup of broth in a saucepan and heat it for one minute until it starts boiling. Slowly add the remaining broth and let it cook until it starts boiling again. The liquid will become thick and creamy because of the corn starch.
5. Put milk, garlic powder, and the puree and stir. Then add the pepper and salt according to taste.
6. Remove it from heat. Put the cheddar cheese and stir until it melts.
7. Servings when it is warm. You can keep the leftovers in the fridge for 3 days.

Nutrition:
Calories: 171, Carbohydrates: 22.5 g, Protein: 14.4 g, Fat: 2.5 g, Saturated Fat: 0.4 g, Polyunsaturated Fat: 2.1 g, Trans Fat: 0 g, Cholesterol: 31 mg, Sodium: 521 mg, Fiber: 4.6 g, Sugar: 3 g

## 66. CREAMY CHICKEN VEGETABLE SOUP

Preparation Time: 10 minutes
Cooking Time: 20 minutes
Servings: 6

Ingredients for 1 person:
- 2 tablespoons olive oil
- ½ cup onions, finely chopped
- ½ cup carrots, thinly sliced or shredded
- ½ cup potatoes, diced
- ½ cup green beans
- ½ cup peas
- 1 cup chicken, finely chopped
- 1 (14 oz.) can chicken broth
- ¼ teaspoon black pepper
- 1¼ cup milk
- 1 (10¾-oz.) can cream of celery soup
- 1 (10¾ oz.) can cream of cheddar cheese soup

Directions:
1. In a large saucepan, heat oil; add onions and carrots; cook and stir until softened, about 5 min.
2. Add potatoes, green beans, peas, chicken, broth, and pepper. Cover, and cook over low heat for 1½ hours, or until vegetables are soft; stir occasionally.

3    Add milk, celery soup, and cheddar cheese soup; stir and continue cooking time until heated throughout.

### Nutrition:
Calories 125, Total fat 3.6 g, Total carbohydrate 15.6 g, Protein 7.6 g

## 67. CLAM CHOWDER
**Preparation Time:** 10 minutes
**Cooking Time:** 35 minutes
**Servings:** 6

### Ingredients for 1 person:
- 1 cup onion, finely chopped
- 3 cups potatoes, diced 2 cups half-and-half
- 1 clove garlic, finely chopped
- 2 slices turkey bacon, cooked and finely crumbled
- 1 teaspoon salt ¼ teaspoon black pepper
- 1 (8 oz.) bottle clam juice
- 2 (7-oz.) cans minced clams
- 3 tablespoons whole flour 1 cup milk

### Directions:
1    Remove starch from potatoes by slicing them and soaking in lukewarm water and straining 4 times.
2    In a large saucepan, combine onion, potatoes, garlic, turkey bacon, salt, pepper, and clam juice; cover and cook on low for 30 min, or until vegetables are soft.
3    In a small bowl, stir flour into milk; mix well.
4    Add flour and milk mixture to a saucepan along with half-and-half and clams with their liquid; stirring constantly, cook over medium heat until chowder thickens to desired consistency.
5    Transfer the mixture to a blender; blend until smooth and return to the saucepan.

### Nutrition:
Calories 163, Total fat 5.83 g, Total carbohydrate 19.01 g, Protein 8.83 g

## 68. CREAM OF BROCCOLI SOUP
**Preparation Time:** 10 minutes
**Cooking Time:** 35 minutes
**Servings:** 6

### Ingredients for 1 person:
- 4 cups broccoli florets
- 1 cup onion, chopped
- 2 cups milk
- 1 tablespoon celery flakes
- 1 garlic clove, chopped
- 1 medium potato, peeled and diced
- 1 (14 oz.) chicken broth
- 1½ cup cheddar cheese, shredded
- ¼ teaspoon thyme
- ½ teaspoon salt
- ¼ teaspoon white pepper

### Directions:
1    In a medium saucepan, add broccoli, onion, celery flakes, garlic, potato, and chicken broth; bring to near boiling; reduce heat, cover and cook over low heat for 30 min, or until vegetables are soft.
2    Transfer cooked vegetables with broth to a blender; blend until smooth. Return blended vegetables to saucepan; add milk, cheese, thyme, salt, and pepper.
3    Continue cooking time over low heat until cheese is melted, stirring constantly.

### Nutrition:
Calories 150, Total fat 7 g, Total carbohydrate 15 g, Protein 5 g

## 69. CHICKEN NOODLE SOUP
**Preparation Time:** 30 minutes
**Cooking Time:** 1 hour
**Servings:** 6-8

### Ingredients for 1 person:
- 1 tablespoon olive or canola oil
- ¾ cup onion, finely chopped
- 2/3 cup carrots, shredded
- 4 cups chicken broth
- 1 tablespoon parsley flakes
- 2 cups water
- 1 tablespoon dried celery flakes
- 1 bay leaf
- 1 teaspoon seasoned salt
- 1 cup cooked chicken, finely chopped
- ¼ teaspoon black pepper, or to taste
- 1½ cup egg noodles, uncooked and broken into 3-inch pieces

### Directions:
1    In a large saucepan, add oil, carrots, and onion, then allow to cook on medium heat until soft, about 5 minutes.

2   Add broth, water, celery flakes, bay leaf, and chicken; cover and cook over low heat for 1 hour, stirring occasionally.

3   Stir in parsley, seasoned salt, pepper, and noodles; cover and continue cooking over low heat for 25 minutes.

4   Remove bay leaf before servings.

### Nutrition:
Calories 220, Total fat 5 g, Total carbohydrate 24 g, Protein 18 g

## 70. CORN AND BLACK BEAN SALAD
by Jean Salas – Traverse City

**Preparation Time:** 30 minutes
**Cooking Time:** 0 minutes
**Servings:** 6

### Ingredients for 1 person:
- ¼ teaspoon pepper
- 2 tablespoons olive oil
- Dash salt
- 1 teaspoon brown sugar or honey
- 1 teaspoon minced garlic
- ¼ cup balsamic vinegar
- 2 tablespoons minced red onion
- ¼ cup chopped parsley
- 2 16-ounce cans drained and rinsed black beans
- 1 cup whole kernel corn

### Directions:
1   Place the parsley, red onion, black beans, and corn in a large bowl and mix everything.

2   Whisk the pepper, salt, honey, garlic, lemon juice, olive oil, and balsamic vinegar. Make sure that all of the seasonings are mixed well.

3   Pour the dressing you just made over the corn and bean mixture.

4   Toss everything and allow the vegetables to marinate for at least 30 minutes before you serve them.

5   This will allow all of the flavors to mix, and the flavor will be a lot more intense. Enjoy.

### Nutrition:
Calories: 155, Fat: 5.3 g, Protein: 3.4 g, Carb: 14.6 g

## 71. SEVEN LAYER MEXICAN SALAD
by Kayla Hammond – New Haven

**Preparation Time:** 20 minutes
**Cooking Time:** 30 minutes
**Servings:** 8

### Ingredients for 1 person:
**Dressing:**
- ¼ teaspoon garlic salt
- ½ teaspoon cumin
- 1 tablespoon olive oil
- 2 limes lime juice
- ½ Jalapeño
- ¼ cup cilantro
- Avocado

**Salad:**
- 2 green onions, chopped
- 1 cup low-fat shredded cheddar cheese
- 1 Diced bell pepper
- 1 Can of drained corn
- 1 Can of drained and rinsed black beans
- 1 cup diced tomatoes
- 2 cups chopped romaine lettuce
- Box of Jiffy cornbread

### Directions:
**Dressing:**

1   Place all ingredients for the dressing in your blender, and pulse until the cilantro is well blended into the avocado, and lime juice.

**Salad:**

1   First, prepare the cornbread according to the directions on the box.

2   Once it has cooked through, set it aside and allow it to cool completely.

3   Once it is cooled, cut the cornbread in half and then break half of it up into little crumbs.

4   Put the crumbled cornbread into the bottom of your dish.

5   Using a trifle dish is best because you will be able to see all of the beautiful layers. You can use any bowl that you want if you don't have a trifle dish.

6   Place half of the romaine lettuce on top of the crumbled cornbread. Make sure you evenly spread it across. This is your second layer.

7   Top the lettuce with half of the black beans, making sure that they are evenly distributed.

8   Add half of the corn evenly on top of the beans.

9   Top the corn with half of the chopped bell peppers.

10  Add half of the tomatoes on top of the bell peppers, making sure they are evenly distributed.
11  Sprinkle half of the cheddar cheese on top of the tomatoes.
12  Now drizzle on half of the salad dressing that you made earlier.
13  Repeat this process, starting with the lettuce through the dressing.
14  To finish the recipe, top everything with the green onions and enjoy.
15  You can reserve the rest of the cornbread for another meal, or you can make another salad. The choice is yours.

**Nutrition:**
Calories: 148, Fat: 8.4 g, Protein: 4 g, Carb: 16.8 g

## 72. CHIPOTLE STEAK SALAD
by Angie J. Oleary – Sioux Falls

Preparation Time: 10 minutes
Cooking Time: 10 minutes
Servings: 4

Ingredients for 1 person:
- ½ cup reduced-fat Cheddar cheese, shredded
- 1 tablespoon chopped cilantro
- ½ sliced avocado
- 1 diced and seeded tomato
- 1 head washed and torn, romaine lettuce
- ½ taco seasoning packet
- 4 lean steaks
- Toppings of choice

Directions:
1  Begin by heating a grill or grill pan to medium. Rub the taco seasoning into the meat, making sure it is well coated. Set this aside to let it marinate.
2  Once your grill is hot, place steaks on the grill and cook for five minutes per side until it reaches your desired doneness.
3  Take off the grill and place it on the cutting board. Allow the meat to rest for about four minutes.
4  While steaks are cooking, wash and tear lettuce. Divide out among four plates.
5  Slice the steaks across the grain and add on top of the lettuce. Add avocado, tomato, and cilantro. Sprinkle with cheese. Use salsa as the salad dressing if you would like to. Enjoy.

**Nutrition:**
Calories: 360, Fat: 25.6 g, Protein: 23.9 g, Carb: 9.5 g

## 73. SOFT MEXICAN CHICKEN SALAD
by Elisabeth Dill – Memphis

Preparation Time: 5 minutes
Cooking Time: 5 minutes
Servings: 2

Ingredients for 1 person:
- 2 teaspoons juice from jarred salsa
- 1 teaspoon taco seasoning
- 1 tablespoon light mayonnaise
- 1 cup canned chicken, drained

Directions:
1  Put the drained chicken in a bowl. Take a fork and break the chicken into small pieces.
2  Add the mayonnaise to the chicken and combine well. Mash the chicken into the mayonnaise with the fork.
3  Add the salsa juice and taco seasoning into the chicken mixture and continue to mash until everything is well combined. Serve and enjoy.

**Nutrition:**
Calories: 180, Fat: 4.8, Protein: 21.9, Carb: 10.9 g

## 74. CAPRESE SALAD BITES
by Melissa Webster – Canton

Preparation Time: 10 minutes
Cooking Time: 15 minutes
Servings: 12

Ingredients for 1 person:
For the Bites:
- 24 Cherry tomatoes
- 12 Mozzarella balls
- 12 fresh basil leaves

For the Balsamic Glaze:
- ½ cup balsamic vinegar
- 2 tablespoons extra-virgin olive oil
- 1 garlic clove, minced
- 1 teaspoon Italian seasoning

Directions
To make the bites:
1  Using 12 toothpicks or short skewers, assemble each with 1 cherry tomato, 1 mozzarella ball, 1 basil leaf, and another tomato.

2   Place on a serving platter or in a large glass storage container that can be sealed.

To make the glaze:

1   In a small saucepan, bring the balsamic to a simmer. Simmer for 15 minutes or until syrupy. Set aside to cool and thicken.

2   In a small bowl, whisk olive oil, garlic, Italian seasoning, and cooled vinegar.

3   Drizzle the olive oil and balsamic glaze over the skewers. Serve immediately or keep in the refrigerator for a tasty snack.

**Nutrition:**
Calories: 39; Total fat: 3 g; Protein: 1 g; Carbohydrates: 3 g; Fiber: 0 g; Sugar: 0 g; Sodium: 11 mg.

## 75. GREEK CHOP-CHOP SALAD
by Dorthy Vazquez - Lancaster

**Preparation Time:** 15 minutes
**Cooking Time:** 0 minutes
**Servings:** 6

**Ingredients for 1 person:**
- 1 medium English cucumber, chopped (2 cups)
- 1 cup halved cherry tomatoes
- 1 red bell pepper, seeded and diced
- ½ red onion, diced
- ½ cup pitted Kalamata olives, roughly chopped
- 1 cup crumbled feta cheese
- ½ cup balsamic dressing

**Directions:**

1.   In a large bowl, toss the cucumber, tomatoes, bell pepper, onion, olives, cheese with the dressing, and serve.

**Nutrition:**
Calories: 173; Total fat: 13 g; Protein: 4 g; Carbohydrates: 10 g; Fiber: 1 g; Sugar: 4 g; Sodium: 883 mg.

## GUIDED MEDITATION 7

Begin in a seated position on the ground or in a chair with your hands in your lap, face up or face down. Sit with your spine straight but not rigid. Gently close your eyes and take a few deep breaths in through your nose and out through your mouth. Scan your body for any tension; breathe into those areas until you feel the stress begin to relax.

Once you are in a relaxed state, begin to breathe into your solar plexus chakra, located just above your navel and below the bottom of your rib cage. Each inhales carries energy from your nostrils to your solar plexus chakra, while each exhale carries the energy back up along your spine and out.

Imagine a ten-petaled yellow lotus flower at your solar plexus chakra; its petals closed tightly. As you breathe, each inhale makes the flower glow more brightly and each exhale opens the petals a little more. Continue breathing into your flower until you feel the full strength of its bloom.

As you feel your solar plexus chakra begin to strengthen and open, begin to chant the solar plexus chakra seed sound, RAM. The vibration of the mantra opens your solar plexus chakra even further, and a bright yellow flame begins to surround the lotus flower, although the flower does not burn. With each repetition of RAM, the flame grows larger and larger until it fills your body with its power, burning away all self-doubt and feelings of helplessness.

Continue with this breathing pattern and visualization until your solar plexus chakra feels alight with the fire of your power. When you are ready to end your meditation, imagine the yellow fire slowly receding from your body until a single bright flame is in the center of your yellow lotus flower. Know that you can call on this flame any time your sense of power and autonomy needs to be re-lit. Release the visualization and take a few deep closing breaths. Wiggle your fingers and toes and stretch your neck from side to side. When you are ready, open your eyes and return to the room.

Do this meditation any time you are feeling powerless are doubting your autonomy.

# PERSONAL NOTES

# PERSONAL NOTES

# CHAPTER 12
# SIDES AND SNACKS

BE PART OF THIS COMMUNITY OF CRAZY INNOVATORS AND SHARE YOUR
UNCONVENTIONAL KNOWLEDGE...BE PART OF ...
FUN CLUB KITCHEN

## 76. STRAWBERRY FROZEN YOGURT SQUARES

**Preparation Time:** 8 Hours
**Cooking Time:** 0 minutes
**Servings:** 8
**Ingredients for 1 person:**
- 1 cup barley & wheat cereal
- 3 cups fat-free strawberry yogurt
- 10 oz. frozen strawberries
- 1 cup fat-free milk
- 1 cup whipped topping

**Directions:**
1. Set a parchment paper on the baking tray.
2. Spread cereal evenly over the bottom of the tray.
3. Add milk, strawberries, and yogurt to the blender, and process into a smooth mixture.
4. Use yogurt mixture to top cereal, wrap with foil, and place to freeze until firm (about 8 hours).
5. Slightly thaw, slice into squares, and serve.

**Nutrition:**
Calories: 188, Fat: 0 g, Carbs: 43.4 g, Protein: 4.6 g

## 77. SMOKED TOFU QUESADILLAS

**Preparation Time:** 20 minutes
**Cooking Time:** 5 minutes
**Servings:** 4
**Ingredients for 1 person:**
- 1 lb. extra firm sliced tofu
- 12 tortillas
- 2 tablespoons coconut oil
- 6 slices cheddar cheese
- 2 tablespoons sundried tomatoes
- 1 tablespoon cilantro
- 5 tablespoons sour cream

**Directions:**
1. Lay one tortilla flat and fill with tofu, tomato, cheese, and top with oil. Repeat for as many as you need.
2. Bake for 5 minutes and remove from flame.
3. Top with sour cream.

**Nutrition:**
Calories: 136, Fat: 6 g, Carbs: 13 g, Protein: 10 g

## 78. ZUCCHINI PIZZA BOATS

**Preparation Time:** 15 minutes
**Cooking Time:** 30 minutes
**Servings:** 2
**Ingredients for 1 person:**
- 2 medium zucchini
- ½ cup tomato sauce
- ½ cup shredded mozzarella cheese
- 2 tablespoons parmesan cheese

**Directions:**
1. Set oven to 350°F.
2. Slice zucchini in half lengthwise and spoon out the core and seeds to form boats.
3. Place zucchini halves skin side down in a small baking dish.
4. Add remaining ingredients inside the hollow center, then set to bake until golden brown and fork-tender (about 30 minutes).
5. Serve and enjoy.

**Nutrition:**
Calories: 214, Fat: 7.9 g, Carbs: 23.6 g, Protein: 15.2 g

## 79. PEAR-CRANBERRY PIE WITH OATMEAL STREUSEL

**Preparation Time:** 30 Minutes
**Cooking Time:** 1 Hour
**Servings:** 6
**Ingredients for 1 person:**

**Streusel:**
- ¾ cup oats
- 1/3 cup stevia
- ½ teaspoon cinnamon
- ¼ teaspoon nutmeg
- 1 tablespoon cubed butter

**Filling:**
- 3 cup cubed pears
- 2 cup cranberries
- ½ cup stevia
- 2½ tablespoons cornstarch

**Directions:**
1. Set oven to 350°F.
2. Combine all streusel ingredients in a food processor and process them into a coarse crumb.

3. Next, combine all filling ingredients in a large bowl and toss to combine.
4. Transfer filling into pie crust, then top with streusel mix.
5. Set to bake until golden brown (about an hour). Cool and serve.

Nutrition:
Calories: 280, Fat: 9 g, Carbs: 47 g, Protein: 1 g

## 80. MACERATED SUMMER BERRIES WITH FROZEN YOGURT

Preparation Time: 2 hours
Cooking Time: 0 minutes
Servings: 4
Ingredients for 1 person:
- 1 cup sliced strawberries
- 1 cup blueberries
- 1 cup raspberries
- 1 tablespoon stevia
- 1 teaspoon orange zest
- 2 tablespoons orange juice
- 1-pint low-fat yogurt

Directions:
1. Add stevia, orange zest, orange juice, and berries to a large bowl.
2. Toss to combine. Set to chill for at least 2 hours.
3. Divide yogurt evenly into 4 serving bowls, top evenly with berry mixture and serve.

Nutrition:
Calories: 133, Fat: 1 g, Carbs: 28.4 g, Protein: 1.3 g

## 81. PUMPKIN PIE SPICED YOGURT

Preparation Time: 10 Minutes
Cooking Time: 5 Minutes
Servings: 2
Ingredients for 1 person:
- 2 cups low-fat plain yogurt
- ½ cup pumpkin puree
- ¼ teaspoon cinnamon
- ¼ teaspoon pumpkin pie spice
- ¼ cup chopped walnuts
- 1 tablespoon honey

Directions:
1. Combine spices with the pumpkin puree in a medium bowl and stir.
2. Stir in yogurt, and divide into 2 serving glasses. Top with honey and walnuts.
3. Serve and enjoy!

Nutrition:
Calories: 208, Fat: 7 g, Carbs: 22 g, Protein: 16 g

## 82. MAPLE-MASHED SWEET POTATOES

Preparation Time: 5 minutes
Cooking Time: 10 minutes
Servings: 2
Ingredients for 1 person:
- 1 lb. sweet potatoes
- 1 cup carrots, thinly sliced
- 2 tablespoons maple syrup
- ¼ teaspoon nutmeg
- ¼ teaspoon fresh ground pepper
- 4 cups water

Directions:
1. Wash and clean sweet potatoes.
2. Peel and cut into small chunks.
3. In a large bowl, pour water and bring to boil.
4. Put carrots and sweet potatoes into it.
5. Reduce heat and continue cooking for about 10 minutes until the carrots and sweet potatoes become soft.
6. Drain the vegetables using a colander and put them into a bowl.
7. Mas the vegetables until it becomes smooth.
8. Sprinkle ground pepper and nutmeg into it and stir.
9. Drizzle maple syrup over it, and stir.

Nutrition:
Calories 212, Fat 4, Carbs 18, Protein 6, Sodium 176

## 83. GARLIC-PARMESAN CHEESY CHIPS

Preparation Time: 2 minutes + 20 minutes to cool
Cooking Time: 7 minutes
Servings: 2
Ingredients for 1 person:
- ¼ cup shredded Parmesan cheese
- ¼ cup shredded sharp Cheddar cheese

- ¼ teaspoon garlic powder
- Dash salt

Directions:
1. Preheat the oven to 400°F. Line a large baking sheet with parchment paper.
2. In a medium mixing bowl, combine the Parmesan cheese, Cheddar cheese, garlic powder, and salt. Mix well.
3. Place 2 teaspoons of the cheese mixture about an inch or two apart on the baking sheet, making 12 chips.
4. Bake for 5 to 7 minutes, or until the chips are golden brown around the edges.
5. Remove from the oven and let sit for 15 to 20 minutes, or until the chips start to crisp.
6. Enjoy.

Nutrition:
Calories: 98; Protein: 8 g; Fat: 7 g; Carbohydrate: 1 g; Fiber: 0 g; Sugar: 0 g; Sodium: 333 mg

## 84. CHEESY BAKED RADISH CHIPS

Preparation Time: 5 minutes
Cooking Time: 35 minutes
Servings: 2
Ingredients for 1 person:
- 1 cup thinly sliced radishes (2 bunches radishes)
- 1 tablespoon extra-virgin olive oil
- 3 tablespoons nutritional yeast flakes
- ¼ teaspoon salt
- Dash freshly ground black pepper (optional)

Directions:
1. Preheat the oven to 375°F. Line a baking sheet with parchment paper.
2. Place the radishes into a small bowl and toss in the oil.
3. In a small cup, mix the nutritional yeast, salt, and pepper (if using).
4. Place the oil-coated radish slices onto the prepared baking sheet in a single layer and lightly sprinkle the nutritional yeast mixture onto each slice.
5. Bake for about 15 minutes, then flip the chips and bake for another 15 minutes. Remove crispy chips, and then continue to bake any remaining chips for a few minutes more at a time, until crispy and golden brown.
6. Serve and enjoy alone or with your favorite low-carbohydrate dip.

Nutrition:
Calories: 99; Protein: 5 g; Fat: 7 g; Carbohydrates: 4 g; Fiber: 2 g; Sugar: 0 g; Sodium: 313 mg

## 85. SAVORY CHEESE BISCUITS

Preparation Time: 5 minutes
Cooking Time: 15 minutes
Servings: 4
Ingredients for 1 person:
- 1 cup almond flour
- ¼ cup shredded Parmesan cheese
- ¼ cup shredded Cheddar cheese
- 2 teaspoons baking powder
- 2 teaspoons garlic powder
- ½ teaspoon salt
- 2 large eggs

Directions:
1. Preheat the oven to 350°F. Line a large baking sheet with parchment paper and set it aside.
2. In a large bowl, add the almond flour, Parmesan cheese, Cheddar cheese, baking powder, garlic powder, and salt. Mix well. Add the eggs and combine.
3. Scoop a heaping tablespoon of the mixture onto the baking sheet. Using a spatula, flatten the batter slightly into about 2-inch circles. Repeat, placing biscuits about an inch apart. This should yield 8 small biscuits.
4. Bake for 15 minutes, or until the top of the biscuits is slightly golden brown. Serve warm.

Nutrition:
Calories: 275; Protein: 15 g; Fat: 23 g; Carbohydrates: 8 g; Fiber: 3 g; Sugar: 1 g; Sodium: 447 mg

## 86. ITALIAN HERB MUFFINS
by Julia Roberts - Bellfountain

Preparation Time: 5 minutes
Cooking Time: 12 minutes
Servings: 4
Ingredients for 1 person:
- Nonstick cooking spray
- 8 tablespoons almond flour
- ¼ cup shredded Parmesan cheese
- 1 large egg
- 1 teaspoon garlic powder
- 1 teaspoon Italian seasoning
- 1 teaspoon baking powder

- ¼ teaspoon salt

**Directions:**
1. Preheat the oven to 350°F. Line a muffin pan, with 4 cupcake liners and spray the liners with nonstick cooking spray.
2. In a large mixing bowl, combine the almond flour, Parmesan cheese, egg, garlic powder, Italian seasoning, baking powder, and salt. Mix well until fully incorporated.
3. Scoop heaping tablespoons of the mixture into the lined cups until all the batter is used.
4. Bake for 12 minutes or until golden brown on the tops. Enjoy warm.

**Nutrition:**
per Serving (1 Muffin): Calories: 128; Protein: 7 g; Fat: 10 g; Carbohydrates: 5 g; Fiber: 2 g; Sugar: 1 g; Sodium: 217 mg

## 87. CHEESY CAULIFLOWER TOTS
by Martin Knowles – Providence

**Preparation Time:** 5 minutes
**Cooking Time:** 15 minutes
**Servings:** 4

**Ingredients for 1 person:**
- 1 cup cauliflower rice
- ½ cup almond flour
- ½ cup shredded mozzarella cheese
- 1 large egg
- 1 tablespoon cornstarch
- ¼ teaspoon salt

**Directions:**
1. Preheat the oven to 400°F. Line a large baking sheet with parchment paper and set it aside.
2. In a large mixing bowl, combine the cauliflower rice, almond flour, mozzarella cheese, egg, cornstarch, and salt. Mix well until fully incorporated.
3. Scoop heaping tablespoons of the mixture onto the baking sheet about an inch apart until all the batter is used. This recipe should make about 16 tots.
4. Bake for 13 to 15 minutes, until crispy and golden brown. Serve and enjoy.

**Nutrition:**
Calories: 152; Protein: 9 g; Fat: 11 g; Carbohydrates: 6 g; Fiber: 2 g; Sugar: 1 g; Sodium: 253 mg

## 88. MOZZARELLA MUSHROOM CAPS
by Miguel Herzog – Downers Grove

**Preparation Time:** 5 minutes
**Cooking Time:** 20 minutes
**Servings:** 4

**Ingredients for 1 person:**
- 12 white mushroom caps
- 4 oz. fresh mozzarella pearls
- 2 tablespoons almond flour
- 1 tablespoon whipped butter
- ½ teaspoon garlic powder
- Dash salt

**Directions:**
1. Preheat the oven to 350°F. Line a baking sheet with parchment paper.
2. Wash the mushrooms and carefully remove the cap from each one. Place the mushrooms onto the lined baking sheet.
3. Place about three mozzarella pearls (about 1 tablespoon) in each mushroom cap.
4. In a small bowl, mix the almond flour, whipped butter, garlic powder, and salt. Sprinkle the mixture on top of each mushroom cap.
5. Bake for about 20 minutes or until the cheese has melted. Enjoy warm.

**Nutrition:**
Calories: 117; Protein: 8 g; Fat: 9 g; Carbohydrates: 4 g; Fiber: 1 g; Sugar: 0.25 g; Sodium: 141 mg

## 89. ALMOND-CRUSTED MOZZARELLA STICKS
by Harry Carter – Minneapolis

**Preparation Time:** 10 minutes + 2 hours to freeze
**Cooking Time:** 6 minutes
**Servings:** 3

**Ingredients for 1 person:**
- 1 tablespoon cornstarch
- 8 tablespoons almond flour
- ½ teaspoon Italian seasoning
- ¼ teaspoon salt
- 2 large eggs
- 6 (1-oz.) light mozzarella sticks
- 1 tablespoon extra-virgin olive oil

**Directions:**

1. Place the cornstarch on a small plate. On a separate small plate, mix the almond flour, Italian seasoning, and salt. Beat the eggs in a small bowl and place them between the two plates.
2. Cut the mozzarella sticks in half. Lightly coat each mozzarella stick in cornstarch, dip, and coat in the egg, and coat well in the almond flour mixture. Coat each mozzarella piece well with the batter to enclose the cheese in the mixture, so it doesn't spread onto the baking sheet while baking. Place each coated mozzarella piece on a large plate. Repeat until all the mozzarella pieces are coated.
3. Cover the plate with plastic wrap and place the mozzarella sticks in the freezer for about 2 hours.
4. Preheat the oven to 400°F. Line a baking sheet with parchment paper.
5. Place the mozzarella pieces about 1-inch apart on the baking sheet. Using a basting brush, coat each side of each mozzarella piece lightly with the oil.
6. Bake for 4 to 6 minutes, until the cheese starts to bubble, and the crust starts to turn slightly golden. Watch closely to make sure the cheese does not start to spread. Enjoy warm.

**Nutrition:**
Calories: 182; Protein: 11 g; Fat: 15 g; Carbohydrates: 4 g; Fiber: 1 g; Sugar: 1 g; Sodium: 311 mg

## 90. ALMOND LIGHT-AS-AIR COOKIES
by Geraldine Burton – Providence

**Preparation Time:** 5 minutes
**Cooking Time:** 10 minutes
**Servings:** 4

**Ingredients for 1 person:**
- 8 tablespoons almond flour
- 1 tablespoon low-sugar vanilla whey protein powder
- 1 tablespoon whipped butter
- 2 teaspoons vanilla extract
- 1 teaspoon baking powder
- 1 teaspoon finely granulated pure cane sugar
- ½ teaspoon stevia or no-calorie sweetener
- ¼ teaspoon salt

**Directions:**
1. Preheat the oven to 350°F. Line a large baking sheet with parchment paper.
2. In a large bowl, combine the almond flour, protein powder, whipped butter, vanilla extract, baking powder, sugar, stevia, and salt and mix well until fully incorporated.
3. Scoop heaping tablespoons of the mixture onto the baking sheet about an inch apart. Using a spatula, flatten the batter slightly into about 2-inch circles. This should yield 8 cookies.
4. Bake for 7 to 9 minutes, or until the edges of cookies are slightly golden brown. Keep a close eye on the cookies since as soon as this happens, you will want to remove the cookies from the oven to prevent overcooking.
5. Allow the cookies to cool slightly before serving.

**Nutrition:**
Calories: 117; Protein: 6 g; Fat: 9 g; Carbohydrates: 5 g; Fiber: 2 g; Sugar: 2 g; Sodium: 288 mg

## GUIDED MEDITATION 8

Sit in a cross-legged posture.

Close your eyes gently.

Keep your spine upright.

If you feel the need, you can use a backrest.

Maintain an upright posture throughout the meditation session.

Keep your shoulders straight and equidistant.

Your neck should also remain straight.

Raise your chin a little upwards towards the sky.

You can place your hands in your lap or on your lap, as you feel comfortable.

During the meditation, you will need to keep your eyes closed.

You may get several thoughts related to your personal and professional life during the meditation.

Do not pay attention to them.

Simply push them aside and pay attention to your breathing.

Your focus should be on your awareness.

This meditation session will help you in finding your spontaneity, vitality, and will. There are times when all starts to look lost. However, the sun rises in the east daily and brings with it new hopes and possibilities. This meditation session will help you rediscover your lost hopes, aspirations, and ambitions.

Sit calmly with your eyes gently closed.

You don't need to think about anything at this moment.

This is the time to relax.

If there are thoughts rushing to your mind, don't worry.

Let them pass.

They don't concern you at the moment.

You are to become a calm and peaceful person at this moment.

No need to think about anything.
No need to focus on sorrow or happiness.
No need to worry about failures and success.
No need to worry about fears of pleasures.
This is the moment to remain still and silent.
You don't need to do anything.
Bring your awareness to your breathing.
Observe your breathing closely.
Inhale Exhale Inhale Exhale Inhale Exhale Inhale Exhale Inhale Exhale
Keep your focus glued to your breathing.
Try to feel every aspect of your breathing.
Is your breathing rapid at the moment?
It will cool down.
Is the air cold or warm?
Can you sense the air entering your nostrils?
Pay attention to this air.
We will now do deep breathing.
Maintain your focus on the breath.
Don't let it wander away.
It may get diverted to some random thoughts.
Do not worry.
Simply acknowledge the thought and bring your attention back to breathing.
Take a slow and deep breath through your nose and count to 7
1.. 2...3....4.....5....6......7......
Now gently hold this breath to the count of 7
1.. 2...3....4.....5....6......7......
Now exhale through your mouth slowly to the count of 8
1.. 2...3....4.....5....6......7......8.......
Excellent!
Repeat once again
Take a slow and deep breath through your nose and count to 7
1.. 2...3....4.....5....6......7......
Now gently hold this breath to the count of 7
1.. 2...3....4.....5....6......7......
Now exhale through your mouth slowly to the count of 8
1.. 2...3....4.....5....6......7......8.......
Wonderful!!
Observe your breathing once again.
Feel the calm in your breathing now.
Take a deep breath.
Feel the breath rising from your nostrils and diving deep inside your lungs.
Follow its path as it travels to your solar plexus chakra.
Feel the breath illuminating the whole solar plexus chakra from inside.
Take a deep breath again.
Feel your breath illuminating the solar plexus chakra once again.
Feel the power this region holds.
Think of the possibilities it holds.
Visualize yourself living a successful life.
Think of all the things you have always wanted to own.
Feel them in your control.
You can get anything you desire.
The solar plexus chakra in your belly burns bright as a star.
It gives you the potential to make anything possible.
You just need to give a big push to anything you want.
It is possible for you to do it once again.
You have made that possible in the past.
You can again make it possible very easily.
You just need to think of it once.
You simply need to make up your mind for it.
You are ready to take on any challenge in this world.
You can face this world head-on.
You are not afraid of challenges.
They give you the motivation to work harder.
Feel the energy building inside you.
Imagine the strength you have.
The power you can exercise.
The influence you can wield.
All this can help you on the way.
You are capable of achieving anything.
Feel the confidence inside you.
Feel the power inside you.
Feel the strength inside you.
Remain in this position and just admire the moment.
Let it fill you with vigor and vitality.
Inhale Exhale Inhale Exhale.
Bring your awareness back to your breathing.
Take a deep breath.

Inhale Exhale Inhale Exhale Inhale Exhale.
Keeping your eyes closed, observe your breathing closely.
Keep your focus on your breathing.
Inhale Exhale Inhale Exhale.
Bring your focus back to breathing.
Feel your breath once again.
Try to feel your surroundings.
Try to feel your limbs without moving them.
Relax.
Sit for a few moments with your eyes closed.
Now, you can open your eyes whenever you wish.

# PERSONAL NOTES

# PERSONAL NOTES

# CHAPTER 13
# POULTRY AND MEAT

BE PART OF THIS COMMUNITY OF CRAZY INNOVATORS AND SHARE YOUR
UNCONVENTIONAL KNOWLEDGE...BE PART OF ...
FUN CLUB KITCHEN

## 91. CREAMY CHICKEN SOUP AND CAULIFLOWER

Preparation Time: 15 minutes
Cooking Time: 40 minutes
Servings: 2
Ingredients for 1 person:
- 1 teaspoon garlic clove, minced
- 1 teaspoon extra virgin olive oil
- ½ yellow onion, diced
- 1 carrot, diced
- 1 celery stalk, diced
- 1 ½ pounds cooked chicken breast, diced
- 2 cups low-sodium chicken broth
- 2 cups of water
- 1 teaspoon fresh ground black pepper
- 1 teaspoon dried thyme
- 2 and ½ cups fresh cauliflower florets
- 1 cup fresh spinach, chopped
- 2 cups nonfat milk

Directions:
1. Place the large soup over medium-high heat and add garlic in olive oil, Sauté for 1 minute.
2. Add onion, carrot, celery and sauté for 3-5 minutes.
3. Add chicken breast, broth, water, pepper, thyme, cauliflower, and simmer over low-medium heat, cover and cook for 30 minutes.
4. Add fresh spinach and stir for 5 minutes.
5. Stir in milk and serve, enjoy!

Nutrition:
Calories 164, Fat 6, Carbs 8, Protein 6, Sodium 123

## 92. GRILLED CHICKEN WINGS

Preparation Time: 15 minutes
Cooking Time: 20 minutes
Servings: 2
Ingredients for 1 person:
- 1 ½ lbs. frozen chicken wings
- Fresh ground black pepper
- 1 teaspoon garlic powder
- 1 cup buffalo

Directions:
1. Pre-heat your grill to 350ºF. Season wings with pepper and garlic powder, and grill wings for 15 minutes per side.
2. Once they are browned and crispy, toss grilled wings in Buffalo wings sauce and olive oil. Enjoy!

Nutrition:
Calories 188, Fat 5, Carbs 16, Protein 8, Sodium 199

## 93. BUFFALO CHICKEN WRAP

Preparation Time: 10 minutes
Cooking Time: 30 minutes
Servings: 2
Ingredients for 1 person:
- 3 cups rotisserie chicken breast
- 2 cups romaine lettuce, chopped
- 1 tomato, diced
- ½ red onion, finely sliced
- ¼ cup buffalo wing sauce
- ¼ cup creamy peppercorn ranch dressing
- Chopped raw celery as for garnish
- 5 small whole-grain low - carb wraps

Directions:
1. Take a large mixing bowl and add chicken, lettuce, tomato, onion, wing sauce, dressing, and celery.
2. Add 1 cup of mixture onto each wrap and foil wrap over the salad.
3. Use a toothpick to secure the wrap, enjoy!

Nutrition:
Calories 133, Fat 6, Carbs 18, Protein 24, Sodium 276

## 94. CHICKEN CAULIFLOWER BOWLS

Preparation Time: 20 minutes
Cooking Time: 12 minutes
Servings: 2
Ingredients for 1 person:
- 1 large head cauliflower, cored
- 1/2 cup chicken stock
- 1 teaspoon butter
- 1/4 cup chopped onion
- 1/4 cup chopped bell pepper
- 1 cup chopped cooked chicken breast
- 1 teaspoon garlic powder

- Salt and freshly ground black pepper, to taste
- 1/4 cup shredded white cheddar cheese

Directions:
1. Pour water into a large saucepan to a depth of about 2 inches. Set steamer basket in saucepan and place cauliflower in the basket. Cover pan and steam over medium heat until cauliflower is soft, 10 to 12 minutes.
2. Meanwhile, heat butter in a medium nonstick skillet and sauté onion and bell pepper until softened, 4 to 5 minutes, stirring frequently. Remove skillet from heat, add cooked chicken and garlic powder, season to taste with salt and pepper, and stir to combine.
3. Carefully remove the cauliflower from the steamer basket and place it in a large bowl. Crumble and lightly mash cauliflower with a fork and season to taste with salt and pepper. Add chicken stock to cauliflower and puree with an immersion blender until smooth, adding more stock if needed.
4. Scoop cauliflower into 4 bowls, top with the chicken mixture, and sprinkle with the grated cheese to serve. Enjoy!

Nutrition:
Calories 312, Fat 6, Carbs 17, Protein 8, Sodium 213

## 95. CHICKEN CAPRESE

Preparation Time: 15 minutes
Cooking Time: 15 minutes
Servings: 2
Ingredients for 1 person:
- 1 lb. boneless skinless chicken breasts
- 2 tablespoons olive oil, divided
- 1 teaspoon garlic powder
- 1 teaspoon onion powder
- 1 teaspoon Italian herb seasoning
- Salt and freshly ground black pepper
- 1/2 cup grated mozzarella cheese
- 1 cup halved cherry tomatoes
- 2 tablespoons balsamic vinegar
- 2 tablespoons sliced fresh basil leaves

Directions:
1. Cut chicken breasts lengthwise into 1" thick slices and brush all over with about 1 tablespoon olive oil. Mix garlic powder, onion powder, and herb seasoning sprinkle over chicken, and season to taste with salt and pepper.
2. Heat remaining 1 tablespoon olive oil in a large nonstick skillet over medium heat and cook chicken until lightly golden brown and no longer pink inside, 8 to 10 minutes, turning as necessary. Sprinkle mozzarella cheese over chicken and cook until cheese is melted, about 1 minute more.
3. Transfer chicken to a serving plate and arrange tomatoes over the chicken. Drizzle balsamic vinegar over chicken, sprinkle with basil, and serve immediately. Enjoy!

Nutrition:
Calories 174, Fat 6, Carbs 8, Protein 12, Sodium 175

## 96. PULLED CHICKEN

Preparation Time: 15 minutes
Cooking Time: 30 minutes
Servings: 2
Ingredients for 1 person:
- 1 small onion, cut into strips
- 1 small bell pepper, strips
- 1 garlic clove, minced
- 1 tablespoon taco seasoning or barbecue spice rub
- 2 boneless skinless chicken breasts

Directions:
1. Arrange onion and bell pepper strips in the bottom of a 3- to 4-quart slow cooker and sprinkle with garlic.
2. Rub chicken breasts all over with taco seasoning and place in a slow cooker.
3. Cover slow cooker, cook the chicken on low until cooked through, and tender for 30 minutes.
4. Remove chicken from the slow cooker and shred with two forks. Add juices from slow cooker to chicken and sprinkle with additional taco seasoning if desired. Serve immediately and enjoy!

Nutrition:
Calories 213, Fat 8, Carbs 18, Protein 13, Sodium 176

## 97. CHICKEN, BARLEY, AND VEGETABLE SOUP

Preparation Time: 15 minutes
Cooking Time: 30 minutes
Servings: 2
Ingredients for 1 person:
- 1 tablespoon extra-virgin olive oil
- 1 teaspoon minced garlic
- 1 large onion, diced
- 2 large carrots, chopped
- 3 celery stalks, chopped

- 1 (14.5 oz.) can diced tomatoes
- ¾ cup pearl barley
- 2½ cups diced cooked chicken, such as leftovers from whole herbed roasted chicken in the slow cooker
- 4 cups low-sodium chicken broth
- 2 cups water
- ½ teaspoon dried thyme
- ½ teaspoon dried sage
- ¼ teaspoon dried rosemary
- 2 bay leaves

Directions:
1. Place a large soup pot over medium-high heat. Sauté the olive oil and garlic for 1 minute.
2. Add the onion, carrots, and celery and sauté until tender, 3 to 5 minutes.
3. Add the tomatoes, barley, chicken, broth, water, thyme, sage, rosemary, and bay leaves.
4. Bring to a simmer, then reduce the heat to medium-low and cook, uncovered, for about 45 minutes. The soup is done when the barley is tender.
5. Remove and discard bay leaves before serving.

Nutrition:
Calories 198, Fat 3, Carbs 32, Protein 8, Sodium 432

## 98. RANCH-SEASONED CRISPY CHICKEN TENDERS

Preparation Time: 10 minutes
Cooking Time: 20 minutes
Servings: 2

Ingredients for 1 person:
- Nonstick cooking spray
- 6 chicken tenderloin pieces (about 1¼ pounds)
- 2 tablespoons whole-wheat pastry flour
- 1 egg, lightly beaten
- ½ cup whole-wheat bread crumbs
- 2 tablespoons grated Parmigiano-Reggiano cheese
- Parsley
- ¾ teaspoon dried dill
- Garlic powder
- ¼ teaspoon dried basil

Directions:
1. Preheat the oven to 425°F.
2. 2. Prepare three small dishes for coating the chicken. Place the flour in one, the egg in the second, and in the last dish, mix the bread crumbs, Parmigiano-Reggiano cheese, parsley, dill, garlic powder, onion powder, basil, and black pepper. 3. Working one at a time, dip each tenderloin into the flour.
4. Shake off any excess, then dip the chicken into the egg.
5. Finally, place the tenderloin in the bread crumbs and press to coat in the mixture. Place on the baking sheet.
6. Bake for about 20 minutes, or until crispy, brown, and cooked through. Serve immediately.

Nutrition:
Calories 213, Fat 6, Carbs 18, Protein 11, Sodium 123

## 99 A. HEALTHY CHICKEN BURGERS (LOW-CARB & PALEO)

Preparation Time: 10 minutes
Cooking Time: 10 minutes

Ingredients:
1 pound ground chicken
1/2 cup of finely diced onion
2 cloves minced garlic
3/4 tsp fine sea salt
1/4 tsp smoked paprika
2 freshly ground black pepper

Directions:
1. Mix the chicken, onion, garlic, salt, paprika, and many black pepper grinds into a large bowl. Divide the mixture into 4 even sections so you can shape patties using a spoon.
2. Wet your hands to make dealing with the mixture simpler (it doesn't stick to wet hands and make a burger patty by rubbing it between your hands. Repeat the remaining mixture until 4 evenly-sized patties are approximately 1 inch thick.
3. Grate the olive oil in a 12-inch skillet and place it on the stove over medium-high heat. k Arrange all four chicken burgers on the skillet and allow 5 minutes to cook them. Turn burgers over and cook for 4 to 5 minutes on the other hand, or when tested with a thermometer, until the burgers reach an internal temperature of 165 degrees F. (You should cut only one in half to make sure that the middle isn't pink too.)
4. Serve your favourite toppings warmly in the grilled burgers. A bun or lettuce wrap can be used! Cooked burgers are maintained in an airtight container to the fridge for up to 3 days or can be frozen for up to 3 months.

## Nutrition:
Calories: 173kcal, Carbohydrates: 2g, Protein: 20g, Fat: 9g, Saturated Fat: 3g, Cholesterol: 98mg, Sodium: 505mg, Potassium: 621mg, Fiber: 1g, Sugar: 1g, Vitamin A: 60IU, Vitamin C: 2mg, Calcium: 14mg, Iron: 0.9mg

## 99 B. GRILLED CHICKEN BREAST

**Preparation Time:** 15 minutes
**Cooking Time:** 20 minutes
**Servings:** 2

### Ingredients for 1 person:
- 1½ pounds frozen chicken breast
- Freshly ground black pepper
- 1 teaspoon garlic powder
- 1 cup buffalo wing sauce, such as Frank's RedHot
- 1 teaspoon extra-virgin olive oil

### Directions:
1. Preheat the grill to 350°F.
2. Season the wings with black pepper and garlic powder. Grill the breasts for 15 minutes per side. They will be browned and crispy when finished.
3. Toss the grilled wings in the buffalo wing sauce and olive oil.
4. Serve immediately.

### Nutrition:
Calories 324, Fat 6, Carbs 19, Protein 11, Sodium 212

## 100. CHICKEN "NACHOS" WITH SWEET BELL PEPPERS

**Preparation Time:** 10 minutes
**Cooking Time:** 25 minutes
**Servings:** 2

### Ingredients for 1 person:
- Nonstick cooking spray
- 1 (1lb.) package mini bell peppers, stemmed, seeded, and halved
- 2 teaspoons extra-virgin olive oil
- ½ onion, minced
- 2 cups cooked shredded chicken breast (see Ingredient tip)
- 1 large tomato, diced
- 1 teaspoon garlic powder
- 1 teaspoon ground cumin
- Paprika
- 1 cup shredded Colby Jack cheese
- ¼ cup sliced black olives
- 3 scallions, finely sliced
- 1 Jalapeño pepper, seeded, thinly sliced (optional)

### Directions:
1. Preheat the oven to 400°F. Coat the foil with the cooking spray.
2. Arrange the bell pepper halves on the baking sheet cut-side up.
3. Heat the olive oil in a large skillet over medium heat. Add the onion and sauté for 1 to 2 minutes, or until tender. Add the chicken, tomato, garlic powder, cumin, and paprika and cook for about 5 minutes, or until the tomato has softened and the chicken is heated through.
4. Spoon 1 heaping tablespoon of the chicken mixture into each mini bell pepper half
5. Top each with the cheese, black olives, scallions, and jalapeño (if used).
6. Bake for 15 minutes, or until cheese has melted and browned
7. Enjoy immediately.

### Nutrition:
Calories 118, Fat 8, Carbs 22, Protein 6, Sodium 178

## 101. JERK CHICKEN WITH MANGO SALSA

**Preparation Time:** 10 minutes
**Cooking Time:** 30 minutes
**Servings:** 2

### Ingredients for 1 person:
- 2 tablespoons extra-virgin olive oil
- 1 lime juice
- 1 tablespoon minced garlic
- 1 teaspoon ground ginger
- Thyme
- ½ teaspoon cinnamon
- ½ teaspoon ground allspice
- ½ teaspoon ground nutmeg
- ¼ teaspoon cayenne pepper
- ¼ teaspoon ground cloves
- 1 teaspoon freshly ground black pepper
- 1 cup Mango Salsa

### Directions:
1. In a gallon-size zip-top freezer bag, put the olive oil, lime juice, garlic, ginger, thyme, cinnamon, allspice, nutmeg,

cayenne, cloves, and black pepper. Tightly seal the bag and gently mix the marinade.

2. Add the chicken breasts to the marinade. Tightly seal the bag and shake to coat the chicken in the marinade.

3. Refrigerate for at least 30 minutes or overnight.

4. Preheat the grill to medium-high heat. Place the chicken on the grill and discard the marinade. Cook the chicken for about 6 minutes on each side or until the breasts are no longer pink in the middle and reach an internal temperature of 165°F. Alternatively, bake the chicken in a preheated 400°F oven for about 25 minutes or until the juices run clear.

5. Let the chicken rest for 5 minutes before slicing. Top the chicken slices with the Mango Salsa.

Nutrition:
Calories 165, Fat 4, Carbs 14, Protein 8, Sodium 212

## GUIDED MEDITATION 9

Sit cross-legged on the floor with your back straight and shoulders down your back. Relax your jaw and neck tension as you release tension in your back down to your hips. Allow your eyes to close softly. If that is uncomfortable for you, find a place not far from your lap to let your gaze gently rest on. Take several deep breaths in and out to help yourself relax in your meditation.

On your next inhale, bring your thoughts to the top of your head. Picture a crown made of lotus flowers glowing on your head in a soft white glow. Take time to look at each petal on the crown, observing the color, texture, and shape of the petals.

As you observe the flowers on the crown, allow the flowers to begin spinning naturally on the top of your head. As it moves, the flowers begin to open, one petal at a time. When one petal falls open, you notice that numerous petals are hidden behind it, and as those all begin to open, even more petals are behind it again. There is no end to the number of petals you see.

As the petals open and the lotus flowers continue to reveal row after row of petals behind the last, the crown spins faster and faster, bathing all your body below it in its light and warmth.

Each breath you take while bathed in this energy will draw you up to the sky above you and also pull you down to the earth beneath you, connected to all things in between. You feel whole, one, and joyful.

When you feel that your crown chakra is fully opened and balanced, bring your thoughts back to the place you are sitting. Open your eyes, if they were closed, and slowly blink a few times. Before you move your body, sit for another few seconds and think about the feelings you have brought up during your meditation. Feel grateful for your connection to your higher power, the Universe, and your authentic self. Bring a soft smile to your lips as you rest in this feeling.

When you are ready, bring movement back into your body slowly, and return to your day.

## 102. CHICKEN WRAP

Preparation Time: 15 minutes
Cooking Time: 30 minutes
Servings: 2
Ingredients for 1 person:
- 3 cups cooked grilled, canned, or rotisserie chicken breast
- 2 cups chopped romaine lettuce
- 1 tomato, diced
- ½ red onion, finely sliced
- ¼ cup rabbit sauce, such as Frank's RedHot
- ¼ cup Creamy Peppercorn Ranch Dressing
- Chopped raw celery (optional)
- 2 small 100% whole-grain low-carb wraps, such as Tumaro's low-carb wraps

Directions:
1. In a large mixing bowl, combine the chicken, lettuce, tomato, onion, wing sauce, dressing, and celery (if using).
2. Place about 1 cup of the mixture onto each wrap.

Nutrition:
Calories 212, Fat 8, Carbs 16, Protein 9, Sodium 328

## 103. LEMONY DRUMSTICKS

Preparation Time: 5 minutes
Cooking Time: 25 minutes
Servings: 2
Ingredients for 1 person:
- 2 teaspoons baking powder
- ½ teaspoon garlic powder
- 8 chicken drumsticks
- 4 tablespoons salted butter, melted
- 1 tablespoon lemon pepper seasoning

Directions:
1. Sprinkle garlic powder and baking powder over drumsticks and rub them into chicken skin.
2. Place drumsticks into the air fryer basket.
3. Cook at 375°F for 25 minutes.

4. Flip the drumsticks once halfway through the cooking time. Remove once cooked.
5. Mix seasoning and butter in a bowl. Add drumsticks to the bowl and toss to coat.
6. Serve.

**Nutrition:**
Calories 175, Fat 6, Carbs 22, Protein 12, Sodium 155

## 104. STUFFED CHICKEN BREAST

**Preparation Time:** 15 minutes
**Cooking Time:** 15 minutes
**Servings:** 2

**Ingredients for 1 person:**
- 1 (6 oz.) boneless, skinless chicken breast
- ¼ medium white onion, peeled and sliced
- ½ green bell pepper, seeded and sliced
- ½ tablespoon oil
- 1 teaspoon chili powder
- ½ teaspoon ground cumin
- ¼ teaspoon garlic powder

**Directions:**
1. Pound chicken to ¼-inch thickness.
2. Place chicken on a flat surface. Place sliced green pepper, onion, and bell pepper on the chicken and roll tightly. Secure with toothpicks.
3. Drizzle with oil and sprinkle with garlic powder, cumin, and chili powder.
4. Place the roll into the air fryer basket.
5. Cook at 350°F for 25 minutes.
6. Serve.

**Nutrition:**
Calories 148, Fat 8, Carbs 24, Protein 17, Sodium 178

## 105. SPICY CHICKEN WINGS

**Preparation Time:** 30 minutes
**Cooking Time:** 12 minutes
**Servings:** 2

**Ingredients for 1 person:**
- 1 lb. chicken wings
- 1 ½ tablespoon butter, melted
- 2 tablespoons hot sauce
- Salt, to taste

For finishing sauce:
- 2 tablespoon hot sauce
- 1 ½ tablespoons butter, melted

**Directions:**
1. Add the chicken wings, hot sauce, butter, and salt to a mixing bowl and mix well.
2. Place marinated chicken wings in the refrigerator for 2 hours. Preheat the air fryer to 400°F.
3. Add chicken wings into the air fryer basket and air fry for 12 minutes.
4. Meanwhile, in a bowl, combine the hot sauce and melted butter.
5. Remove chicken wings from the air fryer and place them in the hot sauce mixture. Toss well to coat.
6. Serve.

**Nutrition:**
Calories 165, Fat 4, Carbs 18, Protein 12, Sodium 322

## 106. PORK SANDWICHES

**Preparation Time:** 1 hour 45 minutes
**Cooking Time:** 9hrs 30 minutes
**Servings:** 2

**Ingredients for 1 person:**
- 1/3 cup ground cumin
- 1/4 cup sugar
- 2 tablespoons onion powder
- 1 tablespoon Kosher salt
- 1/2 teaspoon pepper
- 1 boneless pork shoulder roast (6 to 7 lbs.)
- 2 teaspoons olive oil
- 1 large onion, quartered
- 1 cup dry red wine or beef broth
- 2/3 cup lime juice
- 1/3 cup lemon juice
- 1/3 cup orange juice
- 1 bay leaf
- 1 teaspoon dried cilantro flakes
- 1 teaspoon dried thyme
- 1 teaspoon ground allspice
- 4 teaspoons olive oil

Sandwiches:
- 2 loaves French bread, unsliced (1 lb. each)
- 1/4 cup sweet pickle relish

- 1/4 cup Dijon mustard
- 8 slices Swiss cheese

### Directions:

1. In a small bowl, blend the first 5 ingredients. Slice roast into 3 portions; brush with oil. Rub the meat with the spice mixture; wrap in plastic. Put in the refrigerator, covered, for 24 hours.

2. Combine seasonings, bay leaf, juices, wine, and onion in a large saucepan. Heat to a boil. Decrease the heat; simmer with a cover for 45 minutes. Strain the sauce, removing seasonings and onion.

3. In a large skillet over medium heat, heat oil. Brown all sides of roast; drain. Place in a 6-quart slow cooker. Spread the sauce over the meat. Cook with a cover for 8 to 10 hours on low until meat seems tender. Transfer the roast; let cool slightly. Skim the grease from cooking juices. With 2 forks, shred the pork. Bring the pork back to the slow cooker; heat through.

4. Start preheating the oven to 325°F. Split the bread horizontally. Scoop out bases of loaves, leaving 3/4-inch shells. Spread mustard and relish inside shells. Layer with cheese and meat. Replace tops.

5. Use heavy-duty foil to wrap sandwiches tightly. Arrange on baking sheets. Bake until heated through for 20 to 25 minutes. Slice each crosswise into 12 pieces.

### Nutrition:
Calories 409, Fat 28, Carbs 26, Protein 36, Sodium 432

## 107. EASY CHILI VERDE

**Preparation Time:** 10 minutes
**Cooking Time:** 5hrs 10 minutes
**Servings:** 2

### Ingredients for 1 person:
- 1 boneless pork shoulder roast (4 to 5 lbs.), cut into 1-inch pieces
- 3 cans (10 oz. each) green enchilada sauce
- 1 cup Salsa Verde
- 1 can (4 oz.) chopped green chilies
- 1/2 teaspoon salt
- Hot cooked rice
- Sour cream, optional

### Directions:

1. Mix salt, green chilies, salsa Verde, enchilada sauce, and pork in a 5-quart slow cooker.

2. Cook, while covered for 5 to 6 hours on low or until the pork, becomes tender. Can serve with rice.

3. Add sour cream on top if you like.

### Nutrition:
Calories 287, Fat 2, Carbs 18, Protein 23, Sodium 688

## 108. BEEF CRACK

**Preparation Time:** 10 minutes
**Cooking Time:** 45 minutes
**Servings:** 2

### Ingredients for 1 person:
- 2 lb. beef short ribs, cut flanken-style
- 2 tablespoons white sugar
- 2 tablespoons steak seasoning
- 1/3 cup soy sauce
- 2 tablespoons white vinegar
- 2 tablespoons maple syrup
- 2 tablespoons cayenne pepper
- 2 teaspoons cayenne pepper
- 1 teaspoon sesame oil
- 1/2 teaspoon ground ginger
- 1/2 teaspoon red pepper flakes

### Directions:

1. Rub the steak seasoning and sugar on the short ribs to season.

2. In a small bowl, combine the red pepper flakes, ginger, sesame oil, 2 tablespoons plus 2 teaspoons of cayenne pepper, maple syrup, vinegar, and soy sauce for the marinade.

3. In a big sealable plastic bag, add the marinade. Put in the short ribs. Seal and put in the fridge to marinate for 1 to 4 hours.

4. Set an outdoor grill to medium-high heat and brush oil lightly over the grate.

5. Take the ribs out from the marinade. Cook the ribs in the grill for about 3 minutes on each side until well-browned.

### Nutrition:
Calories 423, Fat 18, Carbs 9, Protein 6, Sodium 890

## 109. PORK POSOLE

**Preparation Time:** 15 minutes
**Cooking Time:** 1 hour
**Servings:** 2

### Ingredients for 1 person:
- 1 lb. pork loin, chopped
- Salt and ground black pepper, to taste

- 1 tablespoon canola oil
- 1 onion, diced
- 2 tablespoons water
- 4 garlic cloves, minced
- 2 Serrano peppers, minced
- 2 teaspoons ground cumin
- 2 teaspoons ground coriander
- 2 cups water
- 2 cups chicken broth
- 1 (14.5 oz.) can diced tomatoes
- 1/4 cup cornmeal
- 2 (15 oz.) cans hominy, drained
- 1/4 cup chopped fresh cilantro
- 1 lime, juiced

**Directions:**
1. Use pepper and salt to season the pork.
2. In a pot, heat the oil to medium-high. Stir and cook the pork in the heated oil for 5-10 minutes until browned. Place the pork on a plate and continue to heat the pot.
3. Turn down the heat to medium-low. Stir and cook 2 tablespoons of water and onion in the hot pot for 5-7 minutes until the onion turns golden brown and soft, and the water has evaporated. Put in coriander, cumin, serrano peppers, and garlic; stir and cook for around a minute until aromatic.
4. Stir tomatoes, chicken broth, and 2 cups of water into the onion mixture. Add in the cornmeal and whisk, allow to simmer on high heat while frequently stirring; use pepper, salt, pork, and hominy to taste. Turn down the heat to medium-low, cook, and occasionally stir for around half an hour until the hominy mixture gets thick and the onion becomes soft. Stir in lime juice and cilantro.

**Nutrition:**
Calories 289, Fat 12, Carbs 18, Protein 6, Sodium 532

## 110. BRAISED BEEF SHORT RIBS

**Preparation Time:** 10 minutes
**Cooking Time:** 1hr 30 minutes
**Servings:** 2
**Ingredients for 1 person:**
- 1/2 cup all-purpose flour for coating
- 2 teaspoons salt
- 1 pinch ground black pepper
- 4 lbs. beef short ribs
- 2 tablespoons vegetable oil
- 1 cup water
- 1 cup stewed tomatoes
- 1 garlic clove, minced
- 6 potatoes, peeled and cubed
- 3 onions, chopped
- 6 carrots, chopped
- 1 1/2 tablespoon all-purpose flour
- 4 tablespoons water

**Directions:**
1. Mix ground black pepper, salt, and 1/2 cup flour in a bowl. In the seasoned flour, turn the ribs. Heat the oil and brown all sides of the ribs well in a Dutch oven or big pot. Put in garlic, tomatoes, and a cup of boiling water. Turn heat to low, put cover, and let simmer for 1 1/2 hour, putting additional water if needed.
2. In the pot, put carrots, onions, and potatoes. Keep simmering for 30 minutes to 1 hour longer, or until every vegetable is soft. Take off vegetables and meat to a serving platter.
3. In another small bowl, dissolve two tablespoons of water and 1 1/2 tablespoon of flour for each cup of liquid left in the pot. Put the mixture in the pot and mix thoroughly until thickened. Put on top of vegetables and meat.

**Nutrition:**
Calories 490, Fat 4, Carbs 26, Protein 26, Sodium 455

## 111. BEEF AND PEPPERS

**Preparation Time:** 10 minutes
**Cooking Time:** 30 minutes
**Servings:** 2
**Ingredients for 1 person:**
- 2 tablespoons vegetable oil
- 1-1/4 lb. beef top round steak or top sirloin steak, cut into 1-inch cubes
- 1 garlic clove, minced
- 1 medium onion, cut into wedges
- 1 medium red bell pepper, seeded and cut into strips
- 1 medium green bell pepper, seeded and cut into strips
- 1 can (10-1/2 oz.) beef broth
- 1/4 cup water
- 3 tablespoons cornstarch
- Salt and pepper to taste
- Hot cooked rice

**Directions:**

1. In skillet, heat oil; on all sides, brown beef. Add garlic; cook for 2 minutes. Add broth, peppers, and onion; cover. Simmer for 20 minutes.
2. Mix cornstarch and water; mix into broth. Mix and cook until gravy is shiny and thick. Add seasonings; serve on hot cooked rice.

Nutrition:
Calories 298, Fat 12, Carbs 26, Protein 18, Sodium 370

## 112. FIESTA PORK SANDWICHES

Preparation Time: 20 minutes
Cooking Time: 8hrs 20 minutes
Servings: 2

Ingredients for 1 person:
- 1 boneless pork shoulder butt roast (3 to 4 lbs.)
- 2/3 cup lime juice
- 1/4 cup water
- 1/4 cup grapefruit juice
- 2 bay leaves
- 12 garlic cloves, minced
- 1 teaspoon salt
- 1 teaspoon chili powder
- 2 tablespoons olive oil
- 1 large onion, thinly sliced
- 12 to 14 sandwich rolls, split

Directions:
1. Slice the roast in half and use a fork to pierce it several times.
2. Mix the next 8 ingredients in a big bowl. Add 1/2 of the marinade into a big sealable plastic bag. Then put the pork into the bag.
3. Seal and flip to coat. Chill overnight and flip occasionally. Cover and chill the remaining marinade.
4. Strain and remove the marinade. Cook the roast in oil in a Dutch oven on medium heat until all sides are browned. Arrange the onion, roast, and reserved marinade in a 5-quart slow cooker.
5. Cook covered for 2 hours. Turn the heat down to low and cook for a further 6-8 hours until the meat is tender. Remove roast and cut into thin slices or shred.
6. Remove the bay leaf. Skim the fat from cooking juices and serve the juices alongside the pork on rolls for dipping.

Nutrition:
Calories 254, Fat 4, Carbs 26, Protein 6, Sodium 455

## 113. FRUITY PORK ROAST
by Ann L. Edinger – Dallas

Preparation Time: 10 minutes
Cooking Time: 30 minutes
Servings: 2

Ingredients for 1 person:
- 1/2 medium lemon, sliced
- 1/2 cup dried cranberries
- 1/3 cup golden raisins
- 1/3 cup unsweetened apple juice
- 3 tablespoons sherry or additional unsweetened apple juice
- 1 teaspoon minced garlic
- 1/2 teaspoon ground mustard
- 1 boneless pork loin roast (3 lbs.)
- 1/2 teaspoon salt
- 1/4 teaspoon pepper
- 1/8 to 1/4 teaspoon ground ginger
- 1 medium apple, peeled and sliced
- 1/2 cup packed fresh parsley sprigs

Directions:
1. Mix the first 7 ingredients in a small bowl and put them aside. Slice the roast in half and top with ginger, pepper, and salt.
2. Move the seasoned pork to a 3-quart slow cooker. Add the fruit mix on top of the roast. Arrange parsley and apple around the roast. Cook while covered for 8-10 hours on low until the meat becomes soft. Move the meat to a serving platter.
3. Let it sit for 10-15 minutes before cutting.

Nutrition:
Calories 321, Fat 21, Carbs 16, Protein 12, Sodium 543

## 114. CRISPY GRILLED PORK
by Bobby Avilla – Florence

Preparation Time: 10 minutes
Cooking Time: 40 minutes
Servings: 2

Ingredients for 1 person:
- 1 lb. pork shoulder, sliced
- 1 tablespoon lemongrass, minced
- ½ tablespoon fish sauce
- 1 ½ teaspoon soy sauce

- 1 tablespoon garlic, minced
- 2 tablespoons sugar
- 2 tablespoons canola oil
- 3 tablespoons onion, minced
- 2 tablespoons fresh parsley, chopped

Directions:

1. In a medium bowl, whisk onions, lemongrass, fish sauce, garlic, oil, soy sauce, and sugar.
2. Add sliced pork into the bowl and mix well, and let marinate for 30 minutes.
3. Place marinated pork slices into the air fryer basket and air fry at 400ºF/200ºC for 10 minutes. Turn halfway through.
4. Garnish with fresh parsley and serve.

Nutrition:
Calories 286, Fat 18, Carbs 20, Protein 6, Sodium 476

## 115. CHICKEN WITH CREAMY MUSHROOM SAUCE
by Wilma Dye – Oak Brook

Preparation time: 10 minutes
Cooking time: 40 minutes

Ingredients:
- bone-in, skin-on chicken thighs
- Kosher salt and freshly ground black pepper, as need
- tbsps. unsalted butter
- tbsps. chopped fresh parsley leaves

FOR THE MUSHROOM SAUCE
- 1 tbsp. unsalted butter
- cloves minced garlic
- ounces cremini thinly sliced mushrooms
- tbsps. all-purpose flour
- 1 1/2 cups of half and half*
- 1/2 tsp dried thyme
- 1/2 tsp dried basil
- Pinch of crushed red pepper flakes
- Kosher salt and freshly ground black pepper, as needed

Directions:

1. Heat the oven to 400 degrees F. Cover the 9 to 13 baking platter with nonstick spray lightly.
2. Season salt and pepper chicken thighs to taste.
3. Melt 2 tbsps of butter on medium heat in a large skillet. Add the chicken, skin-side down, sear both sides, for about 2-3 minutes per side until golden brown.
4. Place the chicken on the skin in one layer in the prepared baking. Set in oven and roast for about 25-30 minutes, until fully cooked, to an inner temperature of 175 degrees F. Excess drain fat.
5. Melt the remaining tbsp. butter in the pot to make the mushroom sauce. Add garlic and champagne and cook, occasionally stirring, for about 5-6 minutes until browned and tender.
6. Whisk in flour, around 1 minute, until lightly browned. Gradually whisk halfway through thyme, basil, and crushed flakes of red pepper; Salt and pepper season as needed. Cook, whisking continuously, for about 3-4 minutes until slightly thickened.
7. Serve chicken with mushroom sauce immediately, garnished with parsley if necessary.

NOTES:

Half and half of both milk and cream are equal parts. You can replace 3/4 cup of whole milk + 1/4 cup of heavy cream, or 2/3 cup skims of low-fat milk + 1/3 cup of heavy cream for 1 and a half cup.

Nutrition:
Calories 270.7 Calories from Fat 189 Total Fat 21.0g Saturated Fat 8.9g Trans Fat 0.2g Cholesterol 87.0mg Sodium 76.8mg Total Carbohydrate 4.6g Dietary Fiber 0.4g Sugars 0.7g Protein 15.9g

## 116. GREEN CHILI SHREDDED PORK
by Donald Todd – Grand Island

Preparation Time: 10 minutes
Cooking Time: 6hrs 10 minutes
Servings: 2

Ingredients for 1 person:
- 1 boneless pork loin roast (3 to 4 lbs.)
- 1-1/2 cups apple cider or juice
- 1 can (4 oz.) chopped green chilies, drained
- 3 garlic cloves, minced
- 1-1/2 teaspoon salt
- 1-1/2 teaspoon hot pepper sauce
- 1 teaspoon chili powder
- 1 teaspoon pepper
- 1/2 teaspoon ground cumin

Directions:

1. Put the pork into a 5- or 6-qt. slow cooker.

2. Combine oregano, cumin, pepper, chili powder, pepper sauce, salt, garlic, green chilies, and mix cider in a small bowl; transfer over the pork.

3. Cook with a cover on low until the meat is tender; 6-8 hours.

4. Take the roast away; let cool slightly. Use two forks to shred.

5. Transfer back to the slow cooker and heat through.

6. Using tongs, serve the pork in tortillas with the toppings of your choice.

**Nutrition:**
Calories 524, Fat 6, Carbs 18, Protein 12, Sodium 650

## 117. BUTTERNUT & PORK STEW
by Herman McCullough – Oak Creek

**Preparation Time:** 10 minutes
**Cooking Time:** 8hrs 20 minutes
**Servings:** 2

**Ingredients for 1 person:**
- 1/3 cup plus 1 tablespoon all-purpose flour, divided
- 1 tablespoon paprika
- 1 teaspoon salt
- 1 teaspoon ground coriander
- 1-1/2 lb. boneless pork shoulder butt roast, cut into 1-inch cubes
- 1 tablespoon canola oil
- 2-3/4 cups cubed peeled butternut squash
- 1 can (14-1/2 oz.) diced tomatoes, undrained
- 1 cup frozen corn, thawed
- 1 medium onion, chopped
- 2 tablespoons cider vinegar
- 1 bay leaf
- 2-1/2 cups reduced-sodium chicken broth
- 1-2/3 cup frozen shelled edamame, thawed

**Directions:**

1. Mix coriander, salt, paprika, and a third cup of flour in the big sealable plastic bag. Put in pork, several pieces at a time, and shake to coat.

2. Brown the pork in oil in batches in the big skillet; drain. Move into the 5-quart slow cooker. Put in the bay leaf, vinegar, onion, corn, tomatoes, and squash. Mix the rest of the flour and broth until smooth in the small-sized bowl; mix in the slow cooker.

3. Keep it covered and cook on low heat until veggies and pork become soft or for 8 to 10 hours. Mix in edamame; keep it covered and cook for half an hour more. Discard the bay leaf.

**Nutrition:**
Calories 254, Fat 4, Carbs 26, Protein 6, Sodium 455

## GUIDED MEDITATION 10

Find a comfortable position, either laying down or sitting. Take in three deep and slow breaths. With each inhale, imagine the breath sending energy to the top of your head. With every exhale, release whatever you are holding in this area, this could be pain or fear or anything else.

Begin to gently tap the top of your head with two fingers. You can also gently massage the area in a circular motion.

As you continue to breathe in and out through your nose, direct your breath to your chakra. Picture a purple glowing light growing and pulsing on the top of your head. For people who identify mostly as male, the light should spin clockwise. For people who identify mostly as female, the light should spin counterclockwise.

As you fall further into your meditative state, talk to your crown chakra to see what it needs. Take some more breaths to notice if you get any feedback. This feedback could be a word, intuition, color, image, song, sound, or feeling. Act upon the feedback you receive. If nothing comes up, you don't need to worry about it. You will get something as you continue to practice.

If you didn't receive a message, but you start to feel a new awareness in your crown chakra, something like a pulsating in this area, you have made a connection to your crown chakra.

As your meditation comes to a close, take three deep and slow breaths. Direct your inhales towards your feet so that you are grounded, and then slowly open your eyes.

Make sure you take things slowly as you start. This will take some time and practice, so be patient. If you end up feeling any pain in your head, you are trying too hard. Take a break and go back to it later.

# PERSONAL NOTES

# PERSONAL NOTES

# CHAPTER 14
# FISH AND SEAFOOD

BE PART OF THIS COMMUNITY OF CRAZY INNOVATORS AND SHARE YOUR
UNCONVENTIONAL KNOWLEDGE...BE PART OF ...
FUN CLUB KITCHEN

## 118. TUNA NOODLE-LESS CASSEROLE

**Preparation Time:** 15 minutes
**Cooking Time:** 40 minutes
**Servings:** 10
**Ingredients for 1 person:**

- Nonstick cooking spray
- 1 medium red onion, chopped
- 1 red bell pepper, chopped
- 1½ cup diced tomato
- 3 cups fresh green beans
- 1/3 cup olive oil-based mayonnaise
- 1 (14.5 oz.) can condensed cream of mushroom soup
- ½ cup low-fat milk
- 1 cup shredded Cheddar cheese
- ½ teaspoon freshly ground black pepper
- 8 (5 oz.) cans water-packed albacore tuna, drained

**Directions:**
1. Preheat the oven to 425°F.
2. Coat a large skillet with the cooking spray and place it over medium heat. Add the onion, red bell pepper, and tomatoes and sauté for about 5 minutes or until the vegetables are tender and the tomatoes start to soften. Remove the skillet from the heat and set it aside.
3. Cut off the stem ends of the green beans, and snap them into 3- to 4-inch pieces.
4. Fill a large saucepot 1/3 full with water, and place a steamer basket inside. Place the pot over high heat, and bring the water to a boil.
5. Add the green beans to the steamer basket, cover the pot, and reduce the heat to medium. Steam the green beans for 5 minutes. Immediately remove them from the heat, drain them, and set them aside.
6. Coat a 9-by-13-inch baking dish with the cooking spray.
7. In a large bowl, mix the mayonnaise, condensed soup, milk, and cheese. Season the mixture with black pepper.
8. Add the tuna, green beans, and sautéed vegetables to the bowl, and mix to combine. Pour the mixture into the baking dish.
9. Serve after baking for 30 minutes and brown.
10. Cooking tip: It's easy to shake up this standby recipe. To boost protein and reduce fat, add ½ cup of nonfat cottage cheese and reduce the mayonnaise to 2 tablespoons. Use an immersion blender to puree until smooth. First, to change the flavor profile, sauté the diced tomatoes in 1 teaspoon of extra-virgin olive oil for 5 minutes before cooking the rest of the vegetables.
11. Set the sautéed tomatoes aside and mix them in with the tuna. Then follow the rest of the directions to put the casserole. The tomatoes become almost sun-dried and help attenuate some of the fishiness of the tuna.

**Nutrition:**

Calories: 147; Total fat: 7 g; Protein: 15 g; Carbs: 6 g; Fiber: 2 g; Sugar: 2 g; Sodium: 318 mg

## 119. SLOW-ROASTED PESTO SALMON

**Preparation Time:** 5 minutes
**Cooking Time:** 20 minutes
**Servings:** 2
**Ingredients for 1 person:**

- 4 (6 oz.) salmon fillets
- 1 teaspoon extra-virgin olive oil
- 4 tablespoons Perfect Basil Pesto

**Directions:**
1. Preheat the oven to 275°F. Brush the foil with olive oil.
2. Place the salmon fillets skin-side down on the baking sheet.
3. Spread 1 tablespoon of pesto on each fillet.
4. Roast the salmon for about 20 minutes, or just until opaque in the center.
5. Serve immediately.

Cooking tip: Enjoy a gourmet meal any night of the week by keeping a bag of freshly frozen wild Alaskan salmon fillets on hand. Look for the kind that is perfectly portioned into individual fillets for easy meal prep—just thaw in the fridge a day or two before needed.

**Nutrition:**

Calories: 182; Total fat: 10 g; Protein: 20 g; Carbs: 1 g; Fiber: 0 g; Sugar: 0 g; Sodium: 90 mg

## 120. HERB-CRUSTED SALMON

**Preparation Time:** 10 minutes
**Cooking Time:** 20 minutes
**Servings:** 2
**Ingredients for 1 person:**

- 2 (4 oz.) salmon fillets
- 2 teaspoons minced garlic
- 1 tablespoon dried parsley
- ½ teaspoon dried thyme

- 2 teaspoons freshly squeezed lemon
- 4 tablespoons grated Parmigiano-Reggiano cheese

Directions:
1. Preheat the oven to 425°F. Line a rimmed baking sheet with parchment paper.
2. Place the salmon skin-side down on the baking sheet and cover with a second piece of parchment paper.
3. Bake for 10 minutes.
4. Meanwhile, mix the garlic, parsley, thyme, lemon juice, and Parmigiano-Reggiano cheese in a small dish.
5. Discard the parchment paper covering the salmon.
6. Use a pastry brush to carefully cover the fillets with the herb-cheese mixture.
7. Bake the salmon, uncovered for about 5 minutes more.
8. The salmon is done when the fish flakes easily with a fork.
9. Serve immediately.

Cooking tip: Don't overcook the salmon. Overcooked fish turns rubbery, and the "fishy" flavor tends to be emphasized. Fish is safely cooked when the internal temperature measures 145°F with a meat thermometer.

Nutrition:
Calories: 197; Total fat: 10 g; Protein: 27 g; Carbs: 9 g; Fiber: 1 g; Sugar: 3 g; Sodium: 222 mg

## 121. BAKED HALIBUT WITH TOMATOES AND WHITE WINE

Preparation Time: 5 minutes
Cooking Time: 35 minutes
Servings: 2

Ingredients for 1 person:
- 3 tablespoons of extra-virgin olive oil
- 1 Vidalia onion, chopped
- 1 tablespoon minced garlic
- 1 (10 oz.) container grape tomatoes
- ¾ cup dry white wine, divided
- 3 tablespoons capers
- 1½ pounds thick-cut halibut fillet, deboned
- ½ teaspoon dried oregano
- Salt
- Freshly ground black pepper

Directions:
1. Preheat the oven to 350°F.
2. In a pan, heat the olive oil. Add the onion and sauté until browned and softened, 3 to 5 minutes.
3. Add the garlic and cook until fragrant, 1 to 2 minutes.
4. Add the tomatoes and cook for 5 minutes, or until they start to soften. Once the tomatoes start to soften, carefully use a potato masher to gently crush the tomatoes just enough to release their juices.
5. Add ½ cup of the wine to the pan and stir. Cook 2 to 3 minutes until slightly thickened. Stir in the capers.
6. Push the vegetables to the sides of the pan, leaving the pan's center open for the fish. Place the fish in the pan and sprinkle it with the oregano, salt, and pepper, then scoop the tomato mixture over the fish.
7. Pour in the remaining ¼ cup of wine.
8. Place in the oven and bake for about 20 minutes, uncovered, or until the fish flakes easily with a fork or reaches an internal temperature of 145°F. Serve.

Nutrition:
Calories: 237; Total fat: 10 g; Protein: 24 g; Carbs: 6 g; Fiber: 1 g; Sugar: 2 g; Sodium: 166 mg

## 122. BAKED COD WITH FENNEL AND KALAMATA OLIVES

Preparation Time: 10 minutes
Cooking Time: 35 minutes
Servings: 4

Ingredients for 1 person:
- 2 teaspoons extra-virgin olive oil
- 1 fennel bulb, sliced paper-thin
- ¼ cup dry white wine
- 1½ cup freshly squeezed orange juice
- 1 teaspoon freshly ground black pepper
- 4 (4 oz.) cod fillets
- 4 slices fresh orange (with rind)
- ¼ cup Kalamata olives pitted
- 2 bay leaves

Directions:
1. Preheat the oven to 400°F.
2. Place a pan on medium heat and add the olive oil. Add the fennel and cook, stirring occasionally, until softened, 8 to 10 minutes.
3. Add the wine. Bring it to a simmer and cook for 1 to 2 minutes. Stir in the orange juice and pepper and simmer for 2 minutes more.

4. Remove the pan from the heat and arrange the cod on top of the fennel mixture. Place the orange slices over the fillets. Position the olives and bay leaves around fish.

5. Roast for 20 minutes or until the fish is opaque. The fish is done when it flakes easily with a fork or reaches an internal temperature of 145°F. Remove the bay leaves before serving.

6. Did You Know? Olives are a great source of heart-healthy fat. Although portion control is key because they can be calorie-dense, olives can bring a pop of flavor to many recipes. Try black olives on a taco salad, Kalamata olives on a Greek-themed pizza or wrap, or place a dish of mixed olives on your charcuterie board for your next dinner party.

**Nutrition:**

Calories: 186; Total fat: 5 g; Protein: 21 g; Carbs: 8 g; Fiber: 3 g; Sugar: 4 g; Sodium: 271 mg

## 123. CUCUMBER TUNA SALAD

**Preparation Time:** 5 minutes
**Cooking Time:** 5 minutes
**Servings:** 6
**Ingredients for 1 person:**

- 2 cans tuna, drained
- 2/3 cup light mayonnaise
- 1 cup cucumber, diced
- 1/2 teaspoon dried dill
- 1 teaspoon fresh lemon juice
- Pepper
- Salt

**Directions:**

1. Add all ingredients into the mixing bowl and mix well.
2. Serve and enjoy.

**Nutrition:**

Calories 215, Fat 13.5 g, Carbohydrates 6.9 g, Sugar 2 g, Protein 16.1 g, Cholesterol 25 mg

## 124. CREAMY SALMON SALAD

**Preparation Time:** 10 minutes
**Cooking Time:** 5 minutes
**Servings:** 2
**Ingredients for 1 person:**

- 6 oz. can salmon, drained
- 1 celery stalk, sliced
- 1 avocado, chopped
- 1/2 bell pepper, chopped
- 2 tablespoons low-fat yogurt
- 2 tablespoons mustard
- 1/4 cup onion, minced

**Directions:**

1. In a mixing bowl, whisk yogurt and mustard.
2. Add remaining ingredients and stir to combine.
3. Serve and enjoy.

**Nutrition:**

Calories 405, Fat 27.8 g, Carbohydrates 17.5 g, Sugar 4.6 g, Protein 24.3 g, Cholesterol 34 mg

## TRATAKA

This third eye meditation exercise should be done in a comfortable place. Do not do this when traveling or in a transit because it would be difficult to concentrate when the body is in motion. Sit in the lotus position and keep your back straight. Close your eyes and inhale, then exhale three times. All you have to do is put all your attention on what is in the middle of your forehead or just around that area. While closing your eyes, draw your eyes to the direction towards that point on your forehead where the third eye is located. After that, silently make a backward count from 100 to 1 while maintaining the direction of your closed eyes toward the center of your forehead.

Upon doing this, you will get a pleasant feeling in your eyes. Although there will be an inevitable strain, you will enjoy the feeling. When you have already finished the backward count, you will start to feel an inexplicable sensation on the location of your third eye. Do not be bothered by this and just concentrate. And once you have already reached the state of stillness, you will start to see your thoughts appear right in front of you. Remain in that state for around 10 to 15 minutes.

Gradually return to the neutral state and get rid of the strain in your eyes. Then slowly get your concentration back from your third eye. Allow ample time for your eyes to get back their normal movements, then inhale and exhale three times. Open your eyes to complete the meditation.

The third eye meditation is also very helpful in enhancing intuitive wisdom. By regularly engaging in this meditation, you can develop intuition.

## 125. BAKED DIJON SALMON

**Preparation Time:** 10 minutes
**Cooking Time:** 10 minutes
**Servings:** 6
**Ingredients for 1 person:**

- 1 lb. salmon

- 3 tablespoons olive oil
- 1 teaspoon ginger, grated
- 2 tablespoons Dijon mustard
- 1 teaspoon pepper
- Salt

Directions:
1. In a small bowl, mix oil, mustard, ginger, and pepper.
2. Preheat the oven to 400ºF/200ºC.
3. Spray a baking tray with cooking spray and set it aside.
4. Place salmon on a baking tray and spread the oil mixture over salmon evenly.
5. Bake salmon for 10 minutes.
6. Serve and enjoy.

Nutrition:
Calories 165, Fat 11.9 g, Carbohydrates 0.7 g, Sugar 0.1 g, Protein 15 g, Cholesterol 33 mg

## 126. BROILED FISH FILLET

Preparation Time: 5 minutes
Cooking Time: 10 minutes
Servings: 2

Ingredients for 1 person:
- 2 cod fish fillets
- 1/8 teaspoon curry powder
- 2 teaspoons butter
- 1/4 teaspoon paprika
- 1/8 teaspoon pepper
- 1/8 teaspoon salt

Directions:
1. Preheat the broiler.
2. Spray broiler pan with cooking spray and set aside.
3. In a small bowl, mix paprika, curry powder, pepper, and salt.
4. Coat fish fillet with paprika mixture and place on broiler pan.
5. Broil fish for 10-12 minutes.
6. Top with butter and serve.

Nutrition:
Calories 224 Fat 5.4 g, Carbohydrates 0.3 g, Sugar 0 g, Protein 41.2 g, Cholesterol 109 mg

## 127. BAKED LEMON TILAPIA
by Jeremy A. Porter – Bergen

Preparation Time: 10 minutes
Cooking Time: 12 minutes
Servings: 4

Ingredients for 1 person:
- 4 tilapia fillets
- 2 tablespoons fresh lemon juice
- 1 teaspoon garlic, minced
- 1/4 cup olive oil
- 2 tablespoons fresh parsley, chopped
- 1 lemon zest
- Pepper
- Salt

Directions:
1. Preheat the oven to 425ºF/220ºC.
2. Spray a baking dish with cooking spray and set it aside.
3. In a small bowl, whisk olive oil, lemon zest, lemon juice, and garlic.
4. Season fish fillets with pepper and salt and place them in the baking dish.
5. Pour olive oil mixture over fish fillets.
6. Bake fish fillets in the oven for 10-12 minutes.
7. Garnish with parsley and serve.

Nutrition:
Calories 252, Fat 14.7 g, Carbohydrates 0.5 g, Sugar 0.2 g, Protein 32.2 g, Cholesterol 85 mg

## 128. GARLIC SHRIMP
by William Gilbreath – Oxnard

Preparation Time: 10 minutes
Cooking Time: 50 minutes
Servings: 8

Ingredients for 1 person:
- 2 lbs. large shrimp, peeled and deveined
- 1 tablespoon parsley, minced
- 1/4 teaspoon chili flakes, crushed
- 1 teaspoon paprika
- 6 garlic cloves, sliced
- 3/4 cup olive oil
- 1/4 teaspoon pepper

- 1 teaspoon kosher salt

Directions:
1. Add all ingredients except shrimp and parsley into the crock pot and stir well.
2. Cover and cook on high for 30 minutes.
3. Add shrimp and stir well.
4. Cover and cook on high for 20 minutes.
5. Garnish with parsley and serve.

Nutrition:
Calories 258, Fat 18.9 g, Carbohydrates 3 g, Sugar 0.1 g, Protein 21.5 g, Cholesterol 162 mg

## 129. CHILI GARLIC SALMON
by Rebecca Benjamin – Burlingame

Preparation Time: 5 minutes
Cooking Time: 2 minutes
Servings: 3

Ingredients for 1 person:
- 1 lb. salmon fillet, cut into three pieces
- 1 teaspoon red chili powder
- 1 garlic clove, minced
- 1 teaspoon ground cumin
- Pepper
- Salt

Directions:
1. Pour 1 1/2 cup water into the instant pot and place trivet into the pot.
2. In a small bowl, mix chili powder, garlic, cumin, pepper, and salt.
3. Rub salmon pieces with spice mixture and place on top of the trivet.
4. Seal the instant pot with a lid and cook on steam mode for 2 minutes.
5. Once done, release pressure using the quick-release method then open the lid.
6. Serve and enjoy.

Nutrition:
Calories 205, Fat 9 g, Carbohydrates 1.1 g, Sugar 0.1 g, Protein 30 g, Cholesterol 65 mg

## 130. AVOCADO SALMON SALAD
by Maria Mariano – Huntington Station

Preparation Time: 10 minutes
Cooking Time: 10 minutes
Servings: 4

Ingredients for 1 person:
Marinade/Dressing:
- 3 tablespoons olive oil
- 2 tablespoons lemon juice fresh squeezed
- 1 tablespoon red wine vinegar (optional)
- 1 tablespoon fresh chopped parsley
- 2 teaspoons garlic minced
- 1 teaspoon dried oregano
- 1 teaspoon salt
- Cracked pepper, as needed
- 1 lb. (500 g) skinless salmon fillets

Salad:
- 4 cups Romaine (or Cos) lettuce leaves, washed and dried
- 1 large cucumber diced
- 2 Roma tomatoes diced
- 1 red onion sliced
- 1 avocado sliced
- 1/2 cup of feta cheese crumbled
- 1/3 cup of pitted Kalamata olives (or black olives), sliced (optional)
- Lemon wedges to serve

Directions:
1. In a big jug, whisk the marinade/dressing ingredients. Into a big, shallow dish, pour out half of the marinade. Refrigerate the remaining marinade that will later be used as the dressing.
2. With the marinade, coat the salmon. Heat 1 tablespoon of oil with medium to high heat in a skillet or grilling pan. Sear both sides of the salmon until crispy and cooked to your taste.
3. Prepare all the salad ingredients while the salmon is cooking, and combine them in a large salad bowl.
4. Slice the salmon and layer the salad over it. Drizzle the remaining untouched dressing with it. Serve with wedges of lemon.

Nutrition:
Calories: 411, Carbohydrates: 12 g, Protein: 28 g, Fat: 27 g, Saturated Fat: 6 g, Cholesterol: 59 mg, Sodium: 128 mg, Potassium: 150 mg, Fiber: 6 g, Sugar: 5 g, Vitamin A: 4755 IU, Vitamin C: 20 mg, Calcium: 166 mg, Iron: 2.4 mg

## 131. SALMON CAKES RECIPE (SALMON PATTIES)
by Robert Horvath – Herndon

**Preparation Time:** 20 minutes
**Cooking Time:** 45 minutes
**Servings:** 4

### Ingredients for 1 person:
- 1 lb. fresh salmon filet
- Garlic Salt - I use Lawry's brand
- Black Pepper
- Olive Oil
- 1 medium onion 1 cup of finely diced
- 1/2 red bell pepper diced
- 1 cup of finely diced
- 3 tablespoons unsalted butter divided
- 1 cup of Panko bread crumbs Japanese Style crumbs
- 2 large eggs lightly beaten
- 3 tablespoons mayo
- 1 teaspoon Worcestershire sauce
- 1/4 cup of minced fresh parsley

### Directions:
1. Preheat the oven to 425°F. Line parchment paper or Silpat on a rimmed baking sheet.
2. Place skin-side down salmon, brush with olive oil, and season with black pepper and garlic salt. Bake for 10-15 min uncovered or only until cooked through (my thinner cut salmon was closer to 10 min).
3. Take it out of the oven and cover it with foil and rest for 10 minutes. Discard the skin, flake the forked salmon, cut any bones, and cool to room temperature.
4. Over medium heat, heat a medium skillet. Add 1 tablespoon of olive oil, 1 tablespoon of butter, and the onion and bell pepper, finely diced.
5. Remove from heat until softened and golden (7-9 minutes).
6. Combine cooled flaked salmon, sautéed onion and pepper, 1 cup of bread crumbs, 1 teaspoon Worcestershire sauce, 1 teaspoon garlic salt, 2 beaten eggs, 3 tablespoons mayonnaise, 1/4 teaspoons black pepper, and 1/4 cup of fresh parsley in a large mixing bowl.
7. Then, stir to combine to form 13-14 patties. Using a flat ice cream scoop, it is easy to portion patties and then press them into 1/3 to 1/2 inch thick patties.
8. Heat 1 tablespoon oil and 1 tablespoon butter with medium heat in a large pan and add half of the salmon cakes until butter is finished sizzling and sauté until golden brown and cooked through.
9. Reduce heat if salmon cakes brown too quickly and remove to a lined paper-towel plate.
10. Add 1 tablespoon of oil and 1 tablespoon of butter and cook the remaining salmon cakes again.

**Nutrition:**
Fat 11 g 17%; Saturated Fat 3 g 19%; Cholesterol 53 mg 18%; Sodium 175 mg 8%; Potassium 221 mg 6%; Carbohydrates 5 g 2%; Fiber 1 g 4%; Sugar 1 g 1%; Protein 9 g 18%; Vitamin A 373 IU 7%; Vitamin C 8 mg 10%; Calcium 21 mg 2%; Iron 1 mg 6%

## 132. SHRIMP CEVICHE
by Sonya Butler – Anchorage

**Preparation Time:** 25 minutes
**Cooking Time:** 20 minutes
**Servings:** 4

### Ingredients for 1 person:
- 2 Serrano chili peppers
- Chopped bunch of cilantro
- Small red onion, chopped
- 4 medium tomatoes
- 1 cup lime juice
- 1 lb. medium raw shrimp

### Directions:
1. Place the lime juice and shrimp in a bowl and toss them. Cover and allow the shrimp to marinate for ten to 15 minutes. The color should change to pink. Don't allow them to marinate for too long; otherwise, the shrimp will become overcooked.
2. Add in the cilantro, chili peppers, tomatoes, and onion.
3. Stir everything gently.
4. Season with some salt.
5. Serve cold.

**Nutrition:**
Calories: 160, Fat: 1 g, Protein: 25 g, Carb: 13 g

## GUIDED MEDITATION 11

Begin by getting comfortable by sitting with your legs crossed, spine straight, and shoulders back.

Place your hands on top of your knees forming the mudra, an 'okay' or 'zero' look-a-like hand gesture by allowing the index and the thumb finger on each hand to touch, or just simply place your palms on your knees making them face upwards.

Start by simply breathing deeply, forming a rhythm with your breath as you inhale and exhale.

Inhale through your nose, hold your breath anywhere from two to three seconds before letting go through your mouth.

Make sure when exhaling, you drag the breath out for another two to three seconds.

Relax your body, each part at a time, like your legs, arms, belly, shoulders, etc.

If you find your mind drifting away, focus on your chest rising with each breath you take and the way it fills and expands your lungs with oxygen. By focusing this way, your mind will become more relaxed and will prevent unnecessary thoughts from emerging when you get further into the meditation.

Once you feel that your mind has settled, then focus on feeling the energy through the ground with each breath you inhale, sensing it more and more.

Let the energy travel up your spine, filling your other chakras with energy, and finally, let it travel to the last region, the crown of your head.

Let that energy gather around like a faint ball of light, floating just above your head.

With the color white to signify purity and spiritual awakening, let that light connect you to the universe.

Picture the bright glow becoming bigger and brighter with each deep breath that you inhale.

Spend some time focusing on this magnificent ball of energy and light, observe how it makes you feel emotionally and physically.

Can you feel overwhelming energy radiating from that ball of light?

Or can you feel tingling sensations or warmth coming from above that area?

At this point in the meditation, you might start to forget about your physical body as you are connecting with that energy on a spiritual level.

Surround yourself with that light, imagine it flowing through your head into your third chakra, then to your throat chakra, and so on until it reaches your root chakra.

Let it rest at each point for a few seconds before moving on to the next chakra point.

Make the energy come back up to the crown at the top of your head.

Let it rest there for a few minutes, glowing and warming up your head before it comes back down to the root chakra and then back up to the crown once more.

The energy should travel up and down three times.

Let the energy flow back through your body to the ground through the bottom of your spine or where your body touches the ground.

Observe any emotions you might feel when the energy was moving up and down or when it left and merged with the ground.

Breathe in deeply for a minute, resting in the sensation of having all your chakras united and opened.

Set an intention to resurface the energy that is already there within your body, ready to be called to healing.

Allow the bright light of your energy to resurface, surrounding your body like an auric field.

Let the light warm your body, purifying your soul and removing any negative impurities that are the cause of all of your troubles and pains.

Center all of that energy into the palms of your hands.

Allow the energy to form a ball of bright and pure light.

Lift your hands upright in front of your chest and form them into a gassho position, the national praying and gratitude gesture.

Draw your life force energy further into your hands and ask the Universe for guidance to be able to heal your mind, getting rid of any bad habits that need to be healed.

Channel the energy in your hands.

Lift your hands as high as you can while still maintaining the gassho position.

Hold the position for a couple of seconds before lowering your hands and placing them one over the other on top of your head, where the crown is.

Feel the tingling sensations and make an intention to open this chakra.

Hold the position for about three minutes before beginning to massage your head with your hands in a circular clockwise motion.

Visualize giving more healing energy to the crown and your subconscious while concentrating on opening the crown and healing the mind, body, and soul.

Get rid of any negative emotions that do not belong within your mind by simply making it the intention for them to vanish.

Breathe in through your nose and out through your mouth. Move your attention to your breathing and imagine that with every breath that you take, the air inside your lungs travels to all different parts of your body that the mind controls, purifying it and granting it the energy it needs to do its day-to-day activities.

Proceed to heal for another three minutes.

As the energy heals the body, keep on breathing deeply as you begin to lightly say the mantra 'om' to help further intensify the healing energy.

Proceed to carry your attention back to the top of your head before slightly moving your hands lower to your temples, engaging with the third eye region for a minute while stimulating the flow of energy.

Return the energy to all of the body, cleansing and purifying it with its powerful energy.

With your eyes still closed, take a deep breath, hold it for five seconds before letting it go with your mouth.

Give your chest the attention that it needs to ensure that the mind is aware of what is going on around it.

Take a minute to let the energy settle down as you normally meditate, keeping your mind from slipping away.

Slowly begin to bring your awareness back into your body by noticing your weight against the physical world before you open your eyes and stay put for another minute.

When the crown chakra is being opened, you might feel like your head is going to explode.

You might get some headaches because the energies are being drawn to you and everything else that is not important is being let go.

When the energy is released, you will feel tingling sensations throughout your body, as well as heat, electricity, and sparks.

Raise your vibrations by doing something that you enjoy and love deeply after the meditation.

Consider taking some time off to relax while letting the energy that you just experienced settle in and continue healing you and your body.

Fish and Seafood | 109

# PERSONAL NOTES

# PERSONAL NOTES

# CHAPTER 15
# DRESSING, SAUCE, SEASONING

BE PART OF THIS COMMUNITY OF CRAZY INNOVATORS AND SHARE YOUR
UNCONVENTIONAL KNOWLEDGE...BE PART OF ...
FUN CLUB KITCHEN

## 133. BABA GANOUSH DIP

**Preparation Time:** 20 minutes
**Cooking Time:** 35 minutes
**Servings:** 6 servings

**Ingredients for 1 person:**
- 2 lbs. Italian eggplants (about 2 medium-sized eggplants)
- 2 medium pressed or minced cloves of garlic
- 2 tablespoons lemon juice, more if necessary
- ¼ cup Tahini
- 1/3 cup extra-virgin olive oil, + more for brushing the eggplant and garnish
- 2 tablespoons chopped fresh flat-leaf parsley, + extra for garnish
- ¾ teaspoon salt, as needed
- ¼ teaspoon cumin powder
- Garnish with a pinch of smoked paprika

Serving suggestions: warmed or toasted pita wedges, bell pepper strips, carrot sticks, cucumber slices, etc.

**Directions:**
1. Heat the oven to 450°F and place a rack in the upper third of the oven. To prevent the eggplant from adhering to the pan, like a big, rimmed baking sheet with parchment paper. Cut the eggplants in half lengthwise and lightly brush the cut sides with olive oil. Place them with the half sides down in the prepared pan.
2. Roast the eggplant for 35-40 minutes, or until the inside is very tender and the skin is collapsing (this might take longer if you are using 1 large eggplant). Allow a few minutes for the eggplant to cool before serving. Turn the eggplants over and use a big spoon to scoop out the meat, leaving the skin remaining.
3. Sift the meat into a mesh strainer set over a mixing bowl, discarding the skins. Remove any stray eggplant skin and throw it away. Allow the eggplant to rest for a few minutes before shaking or stirring it to remove any remaining liquid.
4. Discard the eggplant drippings, then drain and clean off the bowl before adding the eggplant. Toss the eggplant with the garlic and lemon juice and mix vigorously with a fork until the eggplant is broken down. Stir in the tahini until it is completely mixed. Slowly sprinkle in the olive oil while stirring. Stir until the mixture is light and creamy, breaking up any unusually long strings of eggplant with your fork.
5. Combine the parsley, salt, and cumin in a mixing bowl. If you want a more tart flavor, season with more salt (I generally add another ¼ teaspoon) and more lemon juice.
6. Before serving, drizzle just little olive oil over the baba ganoush. Finally, top with parsley and smoked paprika.

Serve with your favorite toppings. It's also delicious on sandwiches!

**Nutrition:**
Total Fat 22.8 g; Sodium 306.7 mg; Total Carbohydrate 11.9 g; Dietary Fiber 5.6 g; Sugars 5.6 g; Protein 3.3 g

## 134. GREEK SALAD DRESSING

**Preparation Time:** 5 minutes
**Cooking Time:** 0 minutes
**Servings:** 6

**Ingredients for 1 person:**
- 1 large finely minced clove garlic
- 1/2 cup extra-virgin olive oil
- 3 tablespoons red wine vinegar
- 1 tablespoon fresh-squeezed lemon juice
- 1/2 teaspoon Dijon mustard
- 1 teaspoon dried oregano
- 1/2 teaspoon salt
- Freshly ground black pepper, as needed.

**Directions:**
1. All of the ingredients should be placed in a jar with a tight-fitting lid. Shake vigorously until the ingredients are fully mixed and emulsified.
2. Season to taste, and if required, add more salt and pepper. (Alternatively, you may combine the ingredients in a mixing bowl, process them in a tiny food processor, or blend them in a blender.)
3. Refrigerate leftovers in a sealed container; bring to room temperature and gently shake before using.

**Nutrition:**
Calories: 163, Fat: 18 g, Sodium: 199 mg, Calcium: 5 mg, Iron: 0.3 mg

## 135. HOMEMADE ENCHILADA SAUCE

**Preparation Time:** 5 minutes
**Cooking Time:** 15 minutes
**Servings:** 4

**Ingredients for 1 person:**
- 1/4 cup vegetable oil
- 1/4 cup all-purpose flour
- 1 (28-ounce) can crushed tomatoes
- 2 tablespoons + 2 teaspoons chili powder
- 1 1/2 teaspoon dried oregano
- 1 teaspoon cumin

- 1 teaspoon garlic powder
- 1 teaspoon onion powder
- 1 tablespoon brown sugar, packed
- Freshly ground black pepper and Kosher salt

**Directions:**

1. Heat the vegetable oil in a pan over medium-high heat. In a large bowl, whisk all the flour and salt for about 1 minute, or until well combined.
2. Sprinkle with salt and pepper, as needed, after adding the tomatoes, chili powder, cumin, garlic powder, oregano, onion powder, brown sugar, and 1 cup of water. Bring to a boil, then lower to low heat and cook for about 10 minutes, or until somewhat thickened.
3. Refrigerate for up to two weeks if stored in an airtight container.

**Nutrition:**

Calories 109.7; Total Fat 7.5 g; Cholesterol 0 mg; Sodium 168.5 mg; Total Carbohydrate 10.6 g; Dietary Fiber 2.0 g; Sugars 4.3 g; Protein 1.7 g

## 136. MANGO SALSA

**Preparation Time:** 15 minutes
**Cooking Time:** 15 minutes
**Servings:** 3 cups

**Ingredients for 1 person:**

- 3 ripe mangos, diced (see photos)
- 1 medium chopped red bell pepper
- ½ cup chopped red onion
- ¼ cup packed freshly chopped cilantro leaves
- 1 seeded and minced jalapeño
- 1 large lime, juiced (about ¼ cup of lime juice)
- 1/8 to ¼ teaspoon salt, as needed

**Directions:**

1. Combine the mango, bell pepper, onion, cilantro, and jalapeño in a serving bowl. Drizzle with one lime juice.
2. Stir the items, using a large spoon. Season with salt as needed, and mix once more. Allow at least 10 minutes for the salsa to rest for the best flavor.

**Nutrition:**

Calories 114; Total Fat 0.7 g; Sodium 100.3 mg; Total Carbohydrate 28.3 g; Dietary Fiber 3.4 g; Sugars 24.5 g; Protein 1.8 g.

## 137. INDIAN SPICED LENTILS
by Wanda L. Pratt – Saginaw

**Preparation Time:** 10 Minutes
**Cooking Time:** 20 Minutes
**Servings:** 4

**Ingredients for 1 person:**

- 2 tablespoons canola oil
- 1 teaspoon ground cumin
- 1 teaspoon ground coriander (5 mL)
- 1 teaspoon turmeric (5 mL)
- 1 or 2 teaspoons red chili flakes
- 1 cup (250 mL) finely chopped onion
- 1 finely chopped celery stalk
- 2 minced garlic cloves
- 1 tablespoon (15 mL) minced fresh ginger
- 1 cup (250 mL) green lentils
- 3 cups (750 mL) water, chicken, or vegetable stock
- 1 tablespoon (15 mL) fresh lemon juice
- Salt and ground black pepper as needed

**Directions:**

1. In a saucepan, heat the oil over medium-high heat. Cook for about 15 seconds, stirring frequently, adding cumin, coriander, and turmeric. Spices should not be burned.
2. Combine the chili flakes, onion, celery, garlic, and ginger in a mixing bowl. Cook for 4 minutes over medium heat or until veggies are soft.
3. Cook for 30 seconds, tossing in the lentils and coating them in the oil and seasonings. Pour in the water or stock, cover, and bring to a boil over high heat.
4. Reduce the heat to low and continue to cook for about 20 minutes, or until the lentils are soft. Sprinkle with salt and pepper as needed after adding the lemon juice.

**Nutrition:**

Calories 250; Total Fat 8 g; Cholesterol 0 mg; Carbohydrates 34 g; Dietary Fiber 9 g; Protein 12 g; Sodium 220 mg; Sugar 3 g; Potassium 515 mg; Folate 15 mcg

## 138. WHITE CHEESE SAUCE
by Kathryn Tomlinson – Florence

**Preparation Time:** 10 minutes
**Cooking Time:** 20 minutes
**Servings:** 20

**Ingredients for 1 person:**

- 1 cup butter

- 3 cups shredded Monterey Jack cheese
- 1 cup sour cream
- 2 cans chopped green chiles, 4 oz., drained

Directions:
1. In a medium saucepan, melt the butter. Set the heat to low and mix in the shredded cheese until it has melted.
2. Cook, stirring periodically, until the sour cream and green chiles are cooked through. Do not allow the water to boil.

Nutrition:
Calories 172; Protein 4.7 g; Carbohydrates 1.2 g; Fat 16.8 g; Cholesterol 44.5 mg; Sodium 293.7 mg

## 139. CITRUS HORSERADISH SAUCE
by Kathryn Perez – Miller

Preparation Time: 5 minutes
Cooking Time: 0 minutes
Servings: 1 Cup

Ingredients for 1 person:
- ½ cup fat-free sour cream
- ½ cup low-fat mayonnaise
- 1 teaspoon grated lemon zest
- 1 tablespoon fresh lemon juice
- 1 teaspoon grated lime zest
- 1 tablespoon fresh lime juice
- 2 teaspoons capers, drained
- 2 teaspoons prepared white horseradish
- ½ cup fresh basil leaves, finely chopped

Directions:
1. Combine all ingredients in a small bowl and whisk until smooth.

Nutrition:
Calories: 37, Fat: 3.0 g, Protein: 1.0 g, Carbs: 2.0 g, Net Carbs: 2.0 g, Fiber: 0 g

## 140. BASIL SAUCE
by Elena Kline – Philadelphia

Preparation Time: 5 minutes
Cooking Time: 0 minutes
Servings: 1 cup

Ingredients for 1 person:
- ½ cup fat-free sour cream
- ½ cup low-fat mayonnaise
- 2 tablespoons prepared horseradish
- ¼ cup chopped fresh basil
- 2 teaspoons light soy sauce
- 2 tablespoons minced onion
- 1 teaspoon minced fresh ginger
- 1 tablespoon anchovy paste

Directions:
1. Combine all ingredients in a medium bowl and mix well.

Nutrition:
Calories: 40, Fat: 3.0 g, Protein: 1.0 g, Carbs: 3.0 g, Net Carbs: 3.0 g, Fiber: 0 g

## 141. PLUM SAUCE
by Bonnie B. Schwab – Fort Leonard Wood

Preparation Time: 0 minutes
Cooking Time: 10 minutes
Servings: 1 cup

Ingredients for 1 person:
- Canola cooking spray
- ½ cup chopped onion
- 3 large red or purple plums, pitted and chopped
- 1 garlic clove, minced
- 1 tablespoon tomato paste
- ½ small Jalapeño pepper, seeded and minced
- 1 tablespoon balsamic vinegar
- 1 tablespoon light soy sauce
- Brown-sugar artificial sweetener (1 teaspoon equivalent)

Directions:
1. Coat a nonstick saucepan with cooking spray, heat over medium-high, and sauté onion until just translucent.
2. Add all other ingredients, lower heat, and cook over low heat for 10 minutes, or until thick.
3. Let cool slightly, pour into a food processor, and blend until smooth.

Nutrition:
Calories: 12, Fat: 0 g, Protein: 0 g, Carbs: 3.0 g, Net Carbs: 3.0 g, Fiber: 0 g

## GUIDED MEDITATION 12

Begin in a comfortable seated position on the ground or a chair with your feet firmly on the ground. Place your hands in your lap, face up to facilitate your ability to receive. Maintain a straight yet relaxed spine. Gently close your eyes and take a few deep breaths in through your nose and out your mouth. Scan your body for any areas of tension and breathe into those areas until they begin to relax.

Once you are in a relaxed state, bring your attention to your crown chakra, located at the very top of your head. Imagine each inhale rising from your nostrils straight up to the crown chakra. Each exhale sends the air back down your spine and out.

Visualize a bright white thousand-petaled lotus sitting atop your crown chakra. Its petals are tightly closed. As you inhale, the flower begins to glow brighter and brighter. As you exhale, its thousand petals slowly begin to open.

Continue to breathe. With each inhale, you feel clear white light, the light of cosmic knowing, pouring into the top of your head through your crown chakra. The light flows down your spine, filling each chakra and your entire body. With each exhale, a similar stream of white light from the lotus streams out of the top of your head, connecting with this ultimate consciousness.

When you are ready to end your meditation, visualize your exhale pulling the white light up through your body, through your crown chakra, and back into the cosmos. Release the visualization and take a few deep closing breaths. Wiggle your fingers and toes and stretch your neck from side to side. When you are ready, open your eyes and return to the room.

Do this meditation any time you are seeking divine connection or higher knowledge.

*Dressing, Sauce, Seasoning*

# PERSONAL NOTES

# PERSONAL NOTES

# CHAPTER 16
# SWEET AND TREATS

BE PART OF THIS COMMUNITY OF CRAZY INNOVATORS AND SHARE YOUR
UNCONVENTIONAL KNOWLEDGE...BE PART OF ...
FUN CLUB KITCHEN

## 142. CHOCOLATE AVOCADO PUDDING

**Preparation Time:** 10 minutes
**Cooking Time:** 10 minutes
**Servings:** 6
**Ingredients for 1 person:**
- 2 avocados, chopped
- ¼ cup creamy almond butter
- 1 teaspoon vanilla
- 1 tablespoon unsweetened cocoa powder
- 1 cup semi-sweet chocolate chips
- 1 cup unsweetened almond milk

**Directions:**
1. Add chocolate chips and almond milk to a microwave-safe bowl and microwave for 30 seconds. Stir well and microwave for 30 seconds more or until chocolate is melted.
2. Add vanilla and cocoa powder and stir well.
3. Pour the chocolate mixture into the blender. Add remaining ingredients and blend until smooth.
4. Pour pudding into the serving bowls and place in the refrigerator for 30 minutes.
5. Serve and enjoy.

**Nutrition:**
Calories 248, Fat 13.4 g, Carbohydrates 28.7 g, Sugar 21.5 g, Protein 3.5 g, Cholesterol 0 mg

## 143. FROZEN BERRY YOGURT

**Preparation Time:** 5 minutes
**Cooking Time:** 5 minutes
**Servings:** 6
**Ingredients for 1 person:**
- 4 cups frozen blackberries
- 1 teaspoon vanilla
- 1 tablespoon fresh lemon juice
- 1 cup full-fat yogurt

**Directions:**
1. Add all ingredients into the blender and blend until smooth.
2. Pour blended mixture into the container. Cover and place in the refrigerator for 2 hours.
3. Serve and enjoy.

**Nutrition:**
Calories 60, Fat 0.9 g, Carbohydrates 11.6 g, Sugar 7 g, Protein 1.8 g, Cholesterol 0 mg

## 144. RASPBERRY SORBET

**Preparation Time:** 5 minutes
**Cooking Time:** 5 minutes
**Servings:** 4
**Ingredients for 1 person:**
- 12 oz. frozen raspberries
- 1 tablespoon honey
- ¼ cup coconut water

**Directions:**
1. Add all ingredients into the blender and blend until smooth.
2. Pour the blended mixture into the container. Cover and place in the freezer for 2-3 hours.
3. Serve and enjoy.

**Nutrition:**
Calories 61, Fat 0.1 g, Carbohydrates 15.5 g, Sugar 13.3 g, Protein 0.4 g, Cholesterol 0 mg

## 145. MIXED BERRY POPSICLES
*by Betty Savarese – Atkinson*

**Preparation Time:** 5 minutes
**Cooking Time:** 5 minutes
**Servings:** 10
**Ingredients for 1 person:**
- 1 cup fresh blackberries
- 1 cup fresh blueberries
- 1 cup fresh raspberries
- 2 tablespoons fresh lemon juice
- 2 cups strawberries, sliced
- 2 tablespoons honey

**Directions:**
1. Add all ingredients into the blender and blend until smooth.
2. Pour the blended mixture into the Popsicle molds and place in the freezer for 4 hours or until set.
3. Serve and enjoy.

**Nutrition:**
Calories 44, Fat 0.3 g, Carbohydrates 10.7 g, Sugar 7.6 g, Protein 0.7 g, Cholesterol 0 mg

## 146. STRAWBERRY YOGURT
*by Gary Mackey – Acton*

**Preparation Time:** 5 minutes

Cooking Time: 5 minutes
Servings: 6
Ingredients for 1 person:
- 1 lb. frozen strawberries
- 1 cup non-fat yogurt
- 1 teaspoon liquid stevia

Directions:
1. Add all ingredients into the blender and blend until smooth.
2. Pour blended mixture into the container.
3. Cover and place in the refrigerator for 2-3 hours.
4. Serve and enjoy.

**Nutrition:**
Calories 87, Fat 0 g, Carbohydrates 19.8 g, Sugar 12 g, Protein 1.8 g, Cholesterol 2 mg

## 147. CHIA SEED PUDDING
by Maria D. Cassady – Corinth

Preparation Time: 5 minutes
Cooking Time: 5 minutes
Servings: 4
Ingredients for 1 person:
- ½ cup chia seeds
- 1 teaspoon liquid stevia
- 1 ½ teaspoon pumpkin pie spice
- ½ cup pumpkin puree
- ¾ cup unsweetened coconut milk
- ¾ cup full-fat coconut milk

Directions:
1. Add all ingredients into the mixing bowl and whisk well to combine.
2. Pour into the serving bowls and place them in the refrigerator for 2 hours.
3. Serve and enjoy.

**Nutrition:**
Calories 275, Fat 24.5 g, Carbohydrates 9.9 g, Sugar 3.3 g, Protein 5.3 g, Cholesterol 0 mg

## 148. AVOCADO HUMMUS
by Maria Hixon – Sorgho

Preparation Time: 10 minutes
Cooking Time: 5 minutes
Servings: 4
Ingredients for 1 person:
- ½ avocado, chopped
- 2 tablespoons olive oil
- ½ teaspoon onion powder
- 1 teaspoon tahini
- ½ teaspoon garlic, minced
- 1 tablespoon lemon juice
- 1 cup frozen edamame, thawed
- Pepper
- Salt

Directions:
1. Add all ingredients into the blender and blend until smooth.
2. Serve with vegetables.

**Nutrition:**
Calories 215, Fat 17 g, Carbohydrates 10 g, Sugar 0.3 g, Protein 9.1 g, Cholesterol 0 mg

## 149. CHOCO PROTEIN BALLS
by Carla Harris – Conway

Preparation Time: 5 minutes
Cooking Time: 10 minutes
Servings: 15
Ingredients for 1 person:
- 1 tablespoon unsweetened cocoa powder
- 1 teaspoon vanilla
- 3 tablespoons pistachios, chopped
- 1/3 cup chia seeds
- 1 cup almond butter
- 1 ½ cup oats

Directions:
1. Line baking tray with parchment paper and set aside.
2. Add all ingredients into the mixing bowl and mix until well combined.
3. Make small balls from the mixture, place them on a prepared tray, and place them in the refrigerator overnight.
4. Serve and enjoy.

**Nutrition:**
Calories 55, Fat 2.4 g, Carbohydrates 6.7 g, Sugar 0.2 g, Protein 2.1 g, Cholesterol 0 mg

## FOCUSED MEDITATION

Find a quiet, safe, and secluded space.

Rest your hands on your knees, with the palms pointed upward.

Close your eyes and begin breathing in and out deeply, relaxing all your muscles completely, one by one, as you do so.

Try to notice any tension and relax.

For the next 3 to 5 minutes, maintain steady breathing, and focus on trying to expand the size and warmth of the red circle.

Eat "grounding" foods.

Changing your diet can be a big part of restoring balance throughout your chakras. The following types of food can help:

Beans, tofu, green peas, and other vegetables and foods rich in protein

Red-colored fruits such as strawberries, cherries, and tomatoes

Root vegetables such as beets, radishes, and potatoes that grow in the earth

Use affirmations.

Chants and affirmations are essential for redirecting your energy as you learn to balance your chakras.

The following are affirmations that have helped many restore balance to the root chakra:

- "Wherever I go, I am always safe and secure."
- "At this moment, I am stable and grounded."
- "I trust that all of my needs for safety and security will be met."
- "I am healthy in body and mind and have abundant life."
- "I am anchored to the earth."
- "I trust the universe to support and guide me."
- "My home is secure and happy."

# CHAPTER 17
# IMPORTANCE OF MINDSET IN CONTROLLING THE DISORDER

Many people suffer from certain mental disorders, which may cause psychosocial difficulties. The way people think can help control whether they will contract a disorder or not. According to the theory of cognitive-behavioral therapy, one's thoughts and behaviors are interconnected. By changing one's behavior or thoughts, it is possible to change their feelings and vice versa. This means that if an individual perceives negative situations in their life as positive, they are more likely to develop a disorder.

Anxiety and depression are a result of thinking that bad things will happen. It has been proven throughout the years by multiple experiments that if someone thinks of a negative event as a positive one, they are more likely to experience anxiety or depression. This will cause many problems, including disruption in their everyday life and physical health.

The majority of those who suffer from anxiety or depression tend not to believe that anything bad will happen to them, making it difficult for them to understand the negative effects of these disorders on their lives. People who are overly concerned with their physical appearance are more likely to develop eating disorders. People who are not able to properly understand the meaning of an event are more likely to experience depression. People who have low self-esteem are more likely to become anxious or depressed. Individuals with certain types of personalities tend to be more susceptible to developing anxiety or depression. For example, people who think they should be treated better than others, or think they should be perfect, tend to develop these disorders. It is proven that the way individuals perceive everyday events will either lead them towards having a disorder or keeping them healthy.

Individuals can control their anxiety and depression through their thoughts and behaviors. When someone is more aware of their thoughts and feelings, they can examine the problem and how it affects them. This is because their thoughts and feelings can be controlled by using certain coping skills. It is proven that when individuals do not let themselves be affected by what other people think, they will better understand themselves and find a solution more easily. Without controlling certain parts of your life you can quickly become anxious or depressed because you will not be able to get rid of unwanted feelings on your own.

## ENDURE DIFFICULTIES WITHOUT LOSING YOUR GRIT

The theory that people with mental disorders are unable to control their thoughts and behaviors is incorrect. There are many ways that individuals can control their thoughts and behaviors. It is proven that people who do not let themselves be influenced by what others think will better understand themselves, what they are doing wrong, and how to change it. If an individual can control his/her thoughts, expressions, emotions, and actions, he/she will be able to learn coping skills that they can use when needed. This encourages people who have anxiety or depression to ignore the things they cannot control so they don't get anxious or depressed about it.

People who suffer from anxiety or depression should understand that they should not let other people bother them too much. If they are not able to accept what others say or do, they should try their best not to think about it too much. This will help them gain control of their emotions and feelings, thus creating a healthy lifestyle. This helps them live a better life without any problems from anxiety or depression.

## RIGHT MINDSET INCREASES CHANCES OF IMPROVEMENT

It is important to have the best mindset possible. This will ensure that you can control your thoughts and emotions, which will help you find ways to better understand your problems. Having the wrong mindset will usually lead people to think that their problems are out of their control, which will cause them to become more anxious or depressed. It is important to understand that people who suffer from anxiety or depression cannot change their situation right away, but by changing the way they think about it, they can gradually improve their situation. People who believe their bad thoughts are uncontrollable are more likely to develop anxiety or depression than those who think they can control them with the right coping skills.

It is important to have the right mindset when you are trying to become healthy. If you are not able to do that, there are certain things that will contribute to breaking it. It is important to understand that the way you think can play a role in your physical health. It is proven that the worse an individual feels about themselves, the worse their physical health will be. Those who suffer from anxiety or depression need to understand this and try their best not to let these feelings get their best. Having a positive mindset about life will help individuals overcome these disorders more quickly than those who have a negative one.

# CHAPTER 18
## HOW TO MANAGE TROUBLESOME SYMPTOMS WITH MEDITATIONS, MINDFULNESS, YOGA, AND EXERCISES ACCORDING TO YOUR PERSONALITY

Do you spend a lot of time and energy trying to control and stop your symptoms, or are they so ingrained in your life that it seems impossible to get through each day without them? If either is the case, you are not alone.

With the help of these simple psychological techniques, you can find peace within yourself by managing troublesome symptom that drains us mentally and physically.

## A. UTILIZE MINDFULNESS TO CONTROL SYMPTOMS

Mindfulness is an ancient Buddhist meditation tool that has been used for thousands of years to achieve peace of mind and tranquility. This technique teaches one to deal with problems without reacting by focusing on the present moment. As a result, you can develop the ability to see patterns in your physical reactions and therefore lessen your symptoms.

With mindfulness techniques, you can control symptoms just by paying attention to them, rather than forcing yourself not to react or become angry. See below about mindfulness exercises.

## B. LEARN HOW YOUR BRAIN AFFECTS SYMPTOMS BY USING MEDITATIONS/MINDFULNESS EXERCISES

An important thing to remember is that the brain you have today is not the same as yesterday because each day, brain cells are regenerating and evolving. In contrast to what we were taught in science class, we now know that we can reshape our brains through meditation and mindfulness.

The good news is that our brains become more resilient and less reactive as we age. It has been found that practicing living mindfully and meditating every day for an hour will help you feel less stressed and more able to cope with your symptoms.

## C. UTILIZE YOGA TO CONTROL SYMPTOMS

Yoga classes help release stress by focusing on breathing techniques, movement of limbs, and meditation. Practicing yoga in a class can help you to focus and master appropriate breathing techniques for many of your symptoms.

## D. LEARN THE PROPER EXERCISES ACCORDING TO YOUR PERSONALITY TYPE AND HOW THEY'LL HELP YOU TO COPE WITH SYMPTOMS.

As mentioned earlier, each person has a different personality type. So it is important to know what types of exercise are best for you so you can understand how the body feels and what to do with it. For example, someone with an INFJ (Introverted, Intuitive, Feeling, Judging) personality type would benefit from:

## 1-EXERCISE: FIND SMALL WAYS TO EMPOWER YOURSELF

Try learning karate, biking, or even hiking for this purpose. Manage symptoms by exploring your surroundings and the world by doing the things you like.

## 2-EXERCISE: USE POSITIVE VISUALIZATION TECHNIQUES

By imagining pleasant, joyful experiences in your mind, you can create an internal image that controls symptoms. For example, if your symptoms are due to stress and pressure, try picturing a part of nature and take deep breaths as you do this.

This will help regulate the number of natural endorphins that we release into our bodies to alleviate symptoms.

## 3-EXERCISE: FIND AN EXERCISE THAT BALANCES YOU

Due to this personality type being one of the most difficult to maintain balance, try using a bicycle or walking for an hour a day.

This will help you focus on the present moment, which helps manage symptoms.

## 4-EXERCISE: HAVE A PROPER DIET TO CONTROL SYMPTOMS

It is important to maintain your weight by eating healthy meals, reducing your refined sugar intake, and portioning out what you eat into smaller portions instead of one big meal. Taking supplements is also suggested for this personality type to help with feelings of depression or being overwhelmed by stress.

## CHOOSE THE RIGHT KIND OF COMPLEMENTARY MENTAL ACTIVITY FOR YOU

Choosing the right kind of complementary mental activity will help you manage your symptoms and achieve a healthier lifestyle. Here are some simple suggestions for those who do not know where to start:

## PACED BREATHING CAN HELP YOU DEAL WITH ANXIETY

Choosing the right kind of complementary mental activity will help you manage your symptoms and achieve a healthier lifestyle. Here are some simple suggestions for those who do not know where to start:

## 1-EXERCISE:

If you just don't feel like exercising, try these simple techniques:

Stretch and do yoga poses first thing in the morning and watch how you can conquer your day.

## 2-EXERCISE:

Try engaging in activities that help you feel good about yourself. For example, volunteering at a local animal shelter or picking up trash on a hike.

## 3-EXERCISE:

Be creative and try to unwind through painting, photography, or playing music.

These activities will help you relax and allow you to become more positive about yourself.

## 4-EXERCISE:

Try some slower-paced activities, like gardening, cooking, or taking piano lessons. These activities will help balance your mind and give you a sense of accomplishment that can help deal with symptoms on an everyday basis.

## 5-EXERCISE:

Help yourself feel good by doing things that interest you. Try getting out of the house and buying new things for yourself, like clothes or a book. These small purchases can help lift your spirits and make you feel more positive about yourself.

## 6-EXERCISE:

Even simple things like having a bubble bath or reading a book can help you relax and feel good about yourself.

Slowly and deeply inhale until your lungs are fully inflated.

Exhale slowly until your lungs are completely empty.

"Deep breathing offers short-term and long-term benefits in reducing stress and anxiety."

# CHAPTER 19
# ILLUSTRATION OF YOGA TECHNIQUES, MINDFULNESS, AND CONCEPTS ON HOW TO INCREASE RESILIENCE

Yoga gives people a solid balance of mindfulness and physical exercise. It's one of the most effective methods to keep your mind healthy and stress levels normal, which boosts your overall quality of life. Yoga also helps you to conquer pain, reconnect with yourself, and focus on what's important. Plus, it trains you in leadership skills so that you can share this practice with others! If you haven't started yet, I highly recommend giving this amazing practice a try. If any individual movement doesn't appeal to you right away, these yoga techniques provide many alternatives so you can master them quickly

Yoga will not only improve your health but also help give back the balance necessary to find that happiness within us all. So how can we do that?

## 1. RELAX INTO THE MOMENT

The first step is to relax into the moment. This means you stop rushing from one thing to another and acknowledge what's going on in front of you. Think about what's actually happening right here, right now, and what you think or feel about it. I find this very useful when I'm about to eat something unhealthy or on the verge of losing my temper! It helps me remain calm and more present in whatever situation I'm facing—and it works almost every time! A personal tool I use for this is a very short version of a meditation exercise called "mindful breathing." It involves paying attention to my breath. If I notice that my mind is wandering from a particular thought or a stressful situation, I pay attention to my breath and empty any negative emotions, thoughts, or worries. Then I focus on the present moment. Through this exercise, you can regain your presence and focus your mind entirely on what's going on right in front of you.

## 2. FOCUS ON THE 'WHYS' NOT JUST THE 'WHATS'

Focusing on what you want out of life is a good way to stay motivated and energized with no regrets when your future self looks back at this time in your life. One of the best ways to stay motivated is to ask yourself "why" you are doing something. It's one of the most powerful tools to help you achieve your goals. When you know why you are doing something, it's far easier to push through any obstacles or challenges that come your way while seeing your true purpose. Giving yourself a reason for why you're moving forward with each decision will make every step count towards your greater goal!

## 3. FIND BALANCE IN ALL THINGS

A lot of us believe that there's only one way to live, act, and make decisions. But the truth is that there are many paths to achieve your goals in life. I'm not saying you shouldn't be yourself or stick to certain rules. What I'm trying to say is that instead of thinking there's only one right path, it's better to take many small "mini-steps" towards your goals. If you have a specific goal in mind, try spending some time exploring other things. Just being around these different experiences every day will help you grow and learn from everything you see or do, making your overall journey much more meaningful and fulfilling!

### 4. FIND THE MEANING BEHIND EACH DECISION

"As for me, I'll do what I want, when I want to." This quote is attributed to The Beatles, but I think it's true in all aspects of our lives. The truth is that everyone has the right to be themselves and follow their path to success. But you have to learn how to manage yourself well for you not to miss an opportunity or risk making a bad decision when you should know better. You can't always take risks because you might end up getting hurt or disappointed in the end! But living your life by finding your purpose is one of the most fulfilling experiences.

## MEASUREMENT CONVERSION

There are two widely employed measuring schemes in nutrition: Metric and US Customary.

### Weight (mass)

| Metric (grams) | US contemporary (ounces) |
|---|---|
| 14 grams | 1/2 ounce |
| 28 grams | 1 ounce |
| 85 grams | 3 ounces |
| 100 grams | 3.53 ounces |
| 113 grams | 4 ounces |
| 227 grams | 8 ounces |
| 340 grams | 12 ounces |
| 454 grams | 16 ounces or 1 pound |

### Volume (liquid)

| Metric | US Customary |
|---|---|
| 0.6 ml | 1/8 tsp |
| 1.2 ml | 1/4 tsp |
| 2.5 ml | 1/2 tsp |
| 3.7 ml | 3/4 tsp |
| 5 ml | 1 tsp |
| 15 ml | 1 tbsp |
| 30 ml | 2 tbsp |
| 59 ml | 2 fluid ounces or 1/4 cup |
| 118 ml | 1/2 cup |
| 177 ml | 3/4 cup |
| 237 ml | 1 cup or 8 fluid ounces |
| 1.9 liters | 8 cups or 1/2 gallon |

### Oven Temperatures

| Metric | US contemporary |
|---|---|
| 121° C | 250° F |
| 149° C | 300° F |
| 177° C | 350° F |
| 204° C | 400° F |
| 232° C | 450° F |

# CONCLUSION

Thank you for making it to the end of this gastric bariatric cookbook. The gastric sleeve operation has become one of the most popular bariatric operations in the United States. More patients are choosing gastric sleeve therapy over other bariatric surgeries because of its effectiveness, low cost, and wide availability among surgeons. Many patients choose the gastric sleeve to lose a substantial amount of weight in a short period. There are many benefits to the bariatric diet. It has the potential to reduce the risk of various health problems, improve quality of life, and can even save lives. This means that you should focus on taking foods that give you the nutritional value that you need. You want to avoid the deficits that can be caused by taking calorie-filled drinks. You also want to avoid taking fried foods, sodas, bread, and grains. You can safely eat lean meats, vegetables, low-fat cottage cheese, fish, and fruits at this stage. Remember that whatever you are taking will be in small quantities. You want to adjust to having a smaller stomach size; you want to refrain from shocking your stomach with too much. This book will help you make better post-operative diet decisions and stay on track with your weight-loss goals. Patients can eat regularly and remain balanced with the help of dietary supplements, minerals, bariatric-friendly meals, and snacks.

You'll feel good while on the way to achieving your targets if you remain stuck to your gastric sleeve diet. It will require dedication and discipline, so you won't have to go it alone. This book guides you through the whole process, from the initial treatment to healing and beyond, and makes a post-surgery diet simple by including healthy choices for all stages of recovery.

If you follow the guidelines, alter your bad behaviors, and replace them with new healthier ones, you should drop more than 60% of your body weight. A bariatric diet is an effective tool for treating obesity and has been proven to improve the lives of millions of people worldwide. For this reason alone, it should be more widely available and promoted as an ideal lifestyle for everyone struggling with their weight and having trouble finding a solution. It's vital to keep in mind that this will only happen if you stick to your surgeon's diet and exercise recommendations. You'll be more likely to keep the weight off in the long run if you make these lifestyle modifications.

Following gastric sleeve surgery, you must adhere to a strict diet to help your body heal and acclimate to the decreased size of your stomach. Also, put the following into consideration:

## CHANGE YOUR DIET

You need to prepare your body for this direction by going on a high-protein liquid diet one or two weeks before your surgery. This will shrink your liver, making the surgery safer for you.

## CHANGE YOUR GROCERY LIST

You need to have a lot of protein-rich liquids before surgery and after surgery. Clear liquids are what you will consume immediately after your surgery for a day or two. After that phase, you will advance to protein shakes and pureed food.

## GET THE CLOTHES YOU WILL NEED

You will need transition clothes for the various weights that you will be. You will want your initial clothing after the surgery to fit loosely. You will also want slip-on shoes so that you won't have to bend over to tie your shoes.

## STOP SMOKING

Surgeons take smoking seriously. Just before surgery, they will likely give you a blood test to see whether you have been smoking lately. If you have, they will cancel your surgery. Why? If you are smoke-free, your recovery will be quicker. You will need to quit smoking one month before your surgery.

## EXERCISE WHEN YOU CAN

Wait about four weeks before you exercise or lift weights so that you will decrease the chance that you will get a hernia in the wound.

## KNOW WHEN TO ASK FOR HELP

Right after your surgery, it will be hard to get anything done. Hopefully, you got your chores done, groceries and meds purchased, food pre-made and frozen, and your helpers lined up before you went into surgery. Don't be afraid to call on the friends and family who agreed to help you when you need them, especially if you notice a complication.

### Good luck!

**A special thanks to for the meditation exercises:**

Leonard Johnson - Saint Louis,/Roxanne Myers - Kearns/ Karin Hamilton - Southfield/Irene Morales - Anniston/ Stan Drouin - Liverpool/Marilu Bloch - Miami

Made in United States
Orlando, FL
30 July 2022